CW01572900

Managing
prisons in a
time of change

Andrew Coyle

Published by

**International Centre
for Prison Studies**
8th Floor
75-79 York Road
London SE1 7AW
United Kingdom

Tel +44 (0) 20 7401 2559
Fax +44 (0) 20 7401 2577
Website: www.prisonstudies.org

ISBN 0-9535221-4-8

Design and print by Intertype

Contents

Foreword

This book is about good prison management in a time of change. It is not based merely on theory and hypothesis; instead it is firmly grounded in hard-earned experience and practical knowledge. Between 1973 and 1997 Andrew Coyle worked as a prison governor, first in the Scottish Prison Service and then in the Prison Service of England and Wales. During that time he governed four prisons. Since 1997 he has been Director of the International Centre for Prison Studies (ICPS) in King's College, University of London, and has worked with prison systems in many regions of the world.

The specific impetus for the book was a project which was carried out between 1998 and 2000 to look at the process of cultural change within the prison environment. The project set out to discover the extent to which there was an ideal model for prison management and, in so far as one was found to exist, to identify the elements of that model. All those immediately involved in this project had direct experience at a senior level in prison management. The project was carried out within a European context but with the expectation that its findings would be relevant to a much wider audience.

Field work for the project consisted of an examination of recent experiences in the management of prisons and prison systems in five different European prison administrations and an identification of comparative lessons. The objective was to describe, explain and analyse successful changes in each of the countries involved and to identify those which had not been successful. The aim was to examine different stages of change in the prison systems involved and to discover what lessons could be learned from they way they were managed.

The members of the project team were:

Per Colliander, former Head of Strategy and International Matters in the Swedish Prison and Probation Service,

Fred Hoogenboom, former Head of Policy in the National Agency of Correctional Institutions in the Netherlands,

Danuta Gajdus, Professor of Law at Torun University and former Deputy Director General of the Polish Prison Service,

Peter Withers, Area Director, Scottish Prison Service,

Andrew Coyle, Director of the International Centre for Prison Studies and former Prison Governor,

Arthur de Frisching, Associate of the International Centre for Prison Studies and former Area Manager, Prison Service England & Wales

They were assisted by Rachel Jones, Tess Kirkby and Guy Laurie, who were at various times seconded from the Prison Service of England & Wales to work in the International Centre for Prison Studies. Important contributions to discussions were also made by Peter Leonard and Niall Clifford of the Prison Service of England & Wales.

Each of the prison systems involved has had to manage a significant change process in recent years. The need to change has been driven by different considerations and pressures in each administration, this has affected the nature of the response. Despite these differences, it is possible to identify several common themes which underlie the change process in each jurisdiction.

England and Wales

The change process in the Prison Service of England and Wales has been influenced considerably by a series of regular organisational reviews, which stretch back in modern times to 1959 at least. Most of them were undertaken following major organisational trauma, such as riots by prisoners or industrial action by staff. Many of these reviews resulted in significant organisational changes. In the course of this project the team set out to analyse this course of events and to discover the present state of affairs.

Netherlands

Throughout much of the period since the end of the Second World War the National Agency of Correctional Institutions in the Netherlands had been regarded by many as a model for other countries. With a rate of imprisonment much lower than the world average, it had been able to deliver good physical conditions, positive regimes and good staff/prisoner relationships. The picture has changed significantly over the last ten years with a dramatic increase in prison numbers, a number of well-publicised escapes by high security prisoners and a loss of public confidence. At the same time the system has had to cope with radical structural change. As part of the project the team examined the implications of these recent changes and tried to find out how the system was responding.

Poland

Throughout the 1990s prison systems in Central and Eastern Europe underwent a period of massive organisational change which reflected wider political events in the region. In some, such as that in Poland, these changes had been foreshadowed in the previous decade. In Poland radical changes were implemented in the prison system largely without any violent reaction from the prisoners or active opposition from staff. The overall pattern of change was so successful that by the end of the 1990s the Polish prison system was held up as an example for Central and Eastern Europe. In some respects developments at that point were in advance of the situation in many Western European jurisdictions.

Sweden

The Prison and Probation Administration in Sweden, along with that in the Netherlands, has traditionally been held up as an example to the rest of Western Europe. Prisons are small and locally based. The prison system is administratively linked with the probation system. Regimes in prisons have had a high therapeutic content. However, in recent years the system has come under increasing pressure because of a number of high profile incidents and gang violence within prisons, and because of the staff reaction to this. The project team wanted to find out how the prison system in Sweden was responding to these new challenges.

Scotland

Following a series of major riots in which staff and prisoners were taken hostage in the late 1980s the Prison Service in Scotland undertook a major organisational review. This was followed by radical changes in the pay and grading arrangements for staff. Throughout the 1990s there was a series of comprehensive surveys among prisoners. The responses influenced many of the subsequent organisational developments. The project examined this process and looked at what lessons might be learned.

The members of the project team are grateful to the Directors General and staff of the prison services which were visited in the course of the project for their generous hospitality and co-operation. They are particularly appreciative of the fact that there was an understanding in each of the services of what the project was trying to achieve. As a consequence, areas of difficulty were openly discussed in addition to those where there had been successful change.

Within the International Centre for Prison Studies, considerable assistance was given by Vivien Francis, Anton Shelupanov, Femke van der Meulen, Helen Fair, Andrew Barclay and Vivien Stern.

The Wates Foundation contributed to the costs of the publication of the English edition of this book. The Constitutional and Legal Policy Institute of the Open Society Institute provided similar funding for the Russian edition. ICPS is extremely grateful to both of these organisations for their generosity.

1. Introduction

Prisons in a time of change

The prison as an institution does not attract a great deal of public attention in the normal course of events. Politicians, the media and the public generally become aware of prisons only when something goes wrong; for example, when a high profile prisoner escapes or when there is a major incident such as a riot. Similarly, discussion about the appropriate use of imprisonment usually only occurs in the aftermath of a high profile crime or when the release of a notorious prisoner is being considered.

Notwithstanding this lack of public attention, prison systems in many countries have undergone a massive process of change over the last twenty years. Between 1980 and 2000 for example, prison administrators in the United States have had to cope with a rise from half a million people in detention to a figure of almost 2 million (United States Bureau of Justice Statistics, 2002). In the countries of the former Soviet Union the infrastructure which supported the system of labour colonies has all but collapsed. Prison administrators in Russia have had to grapple with the seemingly impossible task of providing for one million prisoners in an environment with such a drastic shortage of resources that there is hardly enough money to pay the salaries of staff or to feed the prisoners. Prisons in a number of countries in Latin America have been places of increasing violence and brutality. Problems such as these have been replicated in many countries around the world.

This increasing pressure on prison systems and the difficulty which they have in coping has been the subject of comment by intergovernmental agencies such as the United Nations, through its Special Rapporteur on Torture, and the Council of Europe, through its Committee for the Prevention of Torture and Inhuman or Degrading Treatment or Punishment. They have published a series of reports drawing attention to what is happening in many prison systems around the world. Similarly, non-governmental organisations such as Amnesty International, Human Rights Watch and Penal Reform International have reported on the terrible human rights abuses which have occurred, mainly in regard to prisoners but from time to time also in regard to prison staff.

However, to date little thought has been given to the implications of these developments for prison administrations themselves. How does a prison system cope with a 50% increase in the number of prisoners for which it is responsible when there has been no corresponding increase in resources? Or with a situation in which all previous certainties have vanished and in which there is a lack of clarity about what the system is meant to be achieving? These are major issues for prison management.

And what of the staff who work within these prison systems? In many respects they are a forgotten group of public servants, largely unrecognised in the criminal justice sector. Police have a public profile which ensures that the public is aware of their existence and often they are still regarded as custodians of the peace. Prosecutors are powerful figures in many countries, able to take what may well be life and death decisions about which crimes should be taken to court and which should be dealt with in some other manner. Generally speaking, judges are persons of importance in their communities. The story is quite different in respect to prison staff. They carry out their duties away from the public view. In common with prisoners, they are hidden behind high prison walls. In a disturbing number of countries they are poorly trained, badly paid and are given little respect from their governments, from other public officials or from the rest of society.

In the academic context a significant amount of research has been undertaken into the nature and objectives of imprisonment from legal, judicial and social perspectives (for example, Van Zyl Smit and Dünkel, 2001; Shankardass, 2000). There has also been a limited amount of research into the prison as an institution which needs to be managed (Cressey, 1966; Di Iulio, 1987; Sparks, Bottoms and Hay, 1996). Similarly there has been a restricted amount of analysis of the role of prison staff (Kauffman, 1988; Lombardo, 1989; Liebling and Price, 2001). There has been no real study so far of the dynamics of change in the prison setting, whether from a cultural or an organisational perspective. Yet this is an area which is central to the development of both the prison as an organisation and to the treatment and management of prisoners.

The prison as a dynamic institution

Traditionally prison systems have been regarded, particularly by the staff who work within them, as static and hierarchical organisations. They are seen as static in that their objectives are clear and unchanging. According to this perspective, prisons exist to execute the sentence of the court, which is that the offender should be deprived of his or her liberty. The task of prison staff is to implement that sentence in a decent and humane manner. In so far as this task never changes, the prison system can be described as a static organisation. Secondly, prison systems are hierarchical in that they are disciplined organisations in which orders are passed down from above and the responsibility of staff at lower levels is simply to obey these orders. In a similar manner, prisoners are expected to obey instructions from staff without question. In the prison cliché, "When I tell you to jump, you should not ask 'why?', you should ask 'how high?'". According to this perspective, within the prison setting there are no lines of horizontal communication, only vertical ones; and even these go from the top downwards, never from the bottom upwards.

It has sometimes been argued that this organisational structure is necessary because of the operational demands of prison life. Just as in the armed forces, there is no margin within prisons for failure. The first inflexible requirement is that prisoners must not be allowed to escape. The second is that there must be no disorder within prisons. The only way of ensuring that these two requirements are met is if everyone, staff and prisoners, knows their place in the hierarchy and obeys operational instructions without question.

The attempt to impose such an unyielding structure has had two main consequences. The first has been that many junior staff, who are crucial in determining the culture of a labour intensive organisation like the prison system, have felt undervalued and have not been involved in the change process. The second has been that the bureaucracy of prison systems has usually developed in a highly centralised manner. The story is told of the Chairman of the English Prison Commissioners at the end of the nineteenth century who boasted that he could look at his watch at any time of the day and know exactly what was happening in every prison in the country at that moment. Matters have moved on a bit since those days but in most prison systems there is still an expectation that very little should happen without the approval of the central headquarters. The reality in many countries is quite different from the theory. Prisons often operate on a day to day basis as autonomous units, either because of their geographical distance from the centre of the organisation, as a result of poor communications, or because the governor or director has a high public profile in the local community.

In management terms a static, hierarchical structure can be tolerated when the organisation is stable and not under pressure. In this context the work of the organisation will be predictable, as will be the responsibilities of those working within it and the reactions of those who are affected by it. This is the picture which many long-serving members of staff paint of the prison world in former days. According to this picture, prisons were not subject to external influence by politicians, government officials, the media or the public. The governor or director of the prison acted, according to one's view, as either a father figure or a feudal baron whose main duty consisted in making a daily tour of the prison to ensure that everything and everyone was in its proper place. (In those days all heads of prisons were men.) Prison staff came to work each day, knowing what their tasks would be, in the expectation that they would be left to complete their daily business without interference. Finally, prisoners knew their place and would quietly obey instructions from staff without question. This picture is at best only partly true; at worst it is completely mythical.

Whatever the historical reality, in recent years many prison systems have been described as being in a state of permanent crisis. The suggestion that an organisation is permanently in a state of crisis has grave consequences for its inherent stability and for the confidence of the staff who work in that organisation. This is what has happened in many prison systems. Anyone who has worked at a senior level in prisons in recent years will have heard staff regularly asking, "When is the change going to stop?"; "When are we going to get back to the good old days?"

It is doubtful whether "the good old days" ever existed. Even if one allows that they did, the situation in all prison systems has altered in recent years. Organisational change, sometimes of a radical nature, is a fact of life in all institutions. In respect of prison systems this has implications for the work which staff are expected to undertake and for the type of staff which the organisation wishes to employ. In respect of the staff themselves it is likely to imply a change in the way they approach their daily work and their attitude to prisoners. It may also affect job security for both existing and for new staff, who can no longer look forward to a lifetime guarantee of employment. Many existing staff can be expected to respond positively to the challenge of change. Others may find it impossible to cope, even though they are willing. A third group may simply be unwilling to try. The organisation needs different strategies to deal with all of these responses.

It is possible to develop appropriate response strategies provided it is accepted that prison systems are no longer static hierarchical organisations but are dynamic institutions, subject to continuous change and development. If staff at all levels can be encouraged to recognise this fact, they can be given the opportunity to direct and drive change rather than merely to respond when things go wrong. This will only be possible if there is a change in both the traditional culture and the organisational structure of the prison and the prison system. In the context of what we are concerned with in this study, this means that senior management must be willing to trust junior staff, rather than to assume that they will get things wrong if they are not controlled in all aspects of their work. It also means that junior staff, particularly those who deal directly with prisoners, must be willing to accept responsibility for their actions and to use their initiative in a positive manner when appropriate. There have been a number of examples in recent years, in both individual prisons and national prison systems, where attempts have been made to follow this new model. Some of these have been successful and others less so.

Prisons in an ethical context

One can say that to a certain extent prisons reflect some of the values of the society in which they exist. One instance of this is that societies can choose to make more or less use of imprisonment. Some countries, such as the United States and Russia, have imprisonment rates of almost 700 per 100,000 of their national population. Other countries have much lower rates, with Indonesia for example at 25 per 100,000, Iceland at 30, India at 40 and Finland at 50 (Walmsley, 2002). In some countries imprisonment is used only for those who have committed very serious crimes. Other countries choose to use imprisonment for large numbers of offenders who have committed minor offences, including men and women who are mentally ill, those who are substance abusers and even those who are children or juveniles.

The use that a country makes of imprisonment is likely to affect the internal management of prisons. When prisons are overcrowded and under-resourced management may well be restricted to providing the basic necessities of life for those who are under their care. Simply ensuring that prisoners have sufficient food and clean water, have a bed to sleep on and access to fresh air may be a full time task in some prison administrations. In other jurisdictions there is an attempt to set much higher targets. This may involve doing everything possible to ensure that the damage done to individuals who are imprisoned is kept to a minimum by maintaining family ties and community links. It is also likely to imply encouraging prisoners to face up to the offences which led to their prison sentence and attempting to enhance their personal, social and work skills. All of these activities will be undertaken with the intention of helping prisoners to live law-abiding lives after they are released.

The one consideration, which must never be forgotten in all of this, is that all prisoners are people. To use the recent phrase of one author, they have to be regarded as subjects, not as objects (Duguid, 2000). No matter what crime they may be accused or convicted of, they remain human beings, entitled to respect. This recognition should influence prison staff in the way they carry out all their duties. It is also the foundation stone of good prison management. The details of prison management may vary from country to country since they have to be sensitive to local culture and circumstances. However, the need to operate within an ethical context is universal and is also one of the defining features of good prison management.

This need for an ethical context is the underlying theme of this book. The first chapter emphasises that managing prisons is not easy in any country. It demands a set of professional skills of the highest standard. The argument in the next chapter is that prison management is an important public service which needs to be aware of the organisation of other relevant departments of government. It is also essential that prisons should be organised within a civilian rather than a military structure. If prison management is to be genuinely professional then it cannot be based on the personal preferences of individual managers. The next chapter argues that this is especially true in today's world in which the prison environment is subject to constant change. In a period of change it is important to have an understanding of the history of the prison system, of where it stands at present and to be clear about the direction in which it needs to be taken. If change is inevitable, it is important that it should be managed positively. In that way it can become a positive force rather than something which is presented as a crisis. The next chapter analyses some of the elements of this change process. The outcome of all of this activity will be well-managed prisons. The final chapter in the book considers some issues which provide useful indicators as to whether or not a prison is well managed.

2. Managing prisons: a difficult public profession

Overview

The management of prisons is an intriguing subject for study. There is a wide literature on the theory and practice of management in general and also on the management of large public institutions, such as schools and hospitals, but comparatively little has been written on the management of prisons. This is partly because the world of prisons itself remains relatively closed. It is also because until quite recently it was not acknowledged that there is a particular set of skills required to manage prisons properly.

In some Western countries the management of prisons was originally a responsibility which was given to retired military officers as a means of enhancing their pensions; a task which was mildly interesting but which still allowed plenty of time for other more gentlemanly activities. The work of the prison director could be started in mid-morning and finished by lunchtime, leaving more junior staff to carry out the mundane tasks of seeing to the daily needs of prisoners. Many of the junior prison staff were themselves former service personnel and were at ease with this style of management, which expected little of them other than to maintain a constant routine. In other countries the management of the prison system was, and in some cases such as India remains even today, the responsibility of the police force. A posting to take charge of a prison often came about as an informal sanction as a result of some failing elsewhere. Bright police officers made sure that they completed their spell as a prison manager as quickly as possible before being transferred back to mainstream police duties. There was a variation of this model in the Soviet Union where the prison system was part of the Ministry of the Interior and the senior management of each prison was made up of officers in the Ministry of Interior militia.

Currently in some Western European countries, such as Germany, prison directors must have a legal qualification and their tenure in prisons is but one part of their general training for higher appointments in the public service. In other jurisdictions, such as some parts of the United States, all senior public appointments, including the wardens or directors of jails and prisons, are either themselves subject to election or their appointments are in the gift of elected politicians. In other countries, such as the United Kingdom, prison governors or directors are administrative civil servants, most of whom spend their professional careers working in the prison system.

In the majority of countries there is little concept of prison management as a profession or even a skill which requires specific training and development. A newly appointed prison director is either likely to have previous general legal, administrative or military training or will be expected simply to possess intuitively the skills which are required. This is surprising given the complex nature of many prisons. The biggest prisons in the world, such as Kresty in St Petersburg and Tihar in New Delhi, hold up to 10,000 prisoners, while the smallest may hold no more than a dozen or so prisoners. Managing them requires a specific set of skills, some of which are common to general management and some of which are peculiar to prisons.

This is a particularly opportune moment to undertake a study of prison management. The last twenty years have seen a succession of radical changes in many countries, often of a political nature, which go far beyond the scope of any prison system. This has changed the nature of prison management beyond recognition. In the countries of the former Soviet Union and its allies the whole nature of imprisonment has changed from one which was used to silence critics of the state by use of an extensive network of labour camps. In its place these countries have attempted, some with a greater level of commitment than others, to develop modern prison systems which are used only as places of last resort for society's most serious criminals. In some cases their success in achieving this has been restricted by the demands of politicians and other parts of the criminal justice system, who wish to continue to use imprisonment as a primary tool for criminal investigation or punishment.

A brief review of some of the changes which have taken place over the last twenty years or so, in a number of countries and regions demonstrates some of the complexities of prison management in a modern context.

Poland

The most radical prison reform in Central and Eastern Europe in the second half of the twentieth century took place in Poland. The roots of reform of the Polish prison system preceded the collapse of communism. As a consequence of the imprisonment of political prisoners in the 1950s, groups of students became interested in what was happening in prisons. One result of this was the establishment of "penitentiary circles" of students who were allowed to visit prisons and to talk freely to prisoners. These circles included many people who subsequently became leading figures on the Polish criminal justice and prison scene. After the collapse of communism in 1989 Pavel Moczydlowski, who had been a member of the "penitentiary circles" and was by then a Professor of Sociology at Warsaw University, was invited by the new Solidarity government to become Director General of the prison system (Moczydlowski, 1992). This ushered in a period of fundamental change in the prison system, which in many respects was a reflection of what was happening at that time in the country as a whole.

The process of successful change included several key elements. In the first place, the new Director General and his senior staff had a clear vision of what they wanted to achieve. They were determined to introduce a culture in which prisoners were treated decently and humanely by staff, and in which they were to be given the opportunity to maintain and develop links with family and friends while they were in prison. The new administration was confident that this could be done without placing public security in danger and without sacrificing good order in the prisons. They also knew that if they were to succeed they needed the co-operation of the two key groups of players: the staff and the prisoners.

They set about immediate organisational change, moving quickly from a centralised model to one based on local units. The headquarters organisation was reduced to 180 people. All prisons were divided into 32 regions, with the director of the largest prison leading the region, overseeing the distribution of budgets to other prisons and being responsible for staffing and organisational matters. Legislation introduced at the beginning of 1993 reduced the numbers of regions to 16, with each of them operating within certain parameters as an autonomous system.

Throughout the first years of the new administration senior staff spent a great deal of time explaining their new philosophy, both to gatherings of prison directors and in prisons. Many staff had spent a professional lifetime working to a completely different brief. A significant number found it very difficult to adapt to the new requirements. The Director General understood that it was important that such staff did not suffer for their previous loyalty, provided they had always worked within the rules. For those who wished, arrangements were made for early retirement. Between 1990 and 1991 6,000 out of a total of 21,000 staff left the service on retirement, because either they had reached the appropriate age or they could not cope with the changes which were taking place. By the end of 1992 only 55% of the former staff remained. Those who wished to stay were encouraged to learn to work according to the new dispensation but it was made clear that refusal to do so was not an option.

It has been suggested that one in five prison staff never quite shook off the old mentality.[1] There had always been an underlying difference of approach between staff responsible for security, and case managers who had been introduced throughout the 1980s. The latter dealt directly with the prisoners both as individuals and in groups and were generally much better educated. The former tended to be recruited from the local area and at the time of transition still reported to the Ministry of the Interior rather than the Ministry of Justice. Moczydlowski and his new management team worked unashamedly with the case managers and demanded that security staff follow the new instructions.

As regards prisoners, it was made clear to them that the new arrangements would continue as long as they behaved and would be withdrawn if they misbehaved. The majority of prisoners were ready for this change and accepted that they had to respond positively. Some older prisoners found it difficult to cope. They felt that under the old regime they had known what the rules were but that in the new dispensation they found everything much less clear. Those knowledgeable about prisons will recognise this wish for certainty and consistency, which is common among both staff and prisoners.

The second important element in the change process, according to those who were involved, was that politicians were so busy with other matters that they were not aware of what was happening in the prisons. This was a period of fundamental change in the political landscape of Poland. Moczydlowski and his colleagues had the confidence of their political masters and were left to get on with implementing a comprehensive programme, using a standard set of principles for prison reform.

The third element which contributed to success was linked to the previous one. Because of everything else happening in the country at the time, the media took very little interest in developments in the prison system. In recent years there has been a great deal of media interest in many countries in the way prisons are managed. More often than not, this interest is not positive. It is usually greatest when something has gone wrong, for example an escape or a riot. It will generally be critical of change, which it regards as favourable to the prisoners, relating this to weakness on the part of the authorities. Paradoxically the lack of media interest in Poland persisted even though the new management went out of its way to explain developments to the media.

The final element which contributed to successful change in Poland was the fact that during the period of the most radical change there were no embarrassing incidents, such as scandals, riots or escapes, with the exception of a short period at its beginning when there was some prisoner unrest. Had any of these occurred there may well have been a public outcry and any incident, whatever its real cause, would have been attributed to the changes which were being introduced. At one level, this might be seen merely as fortunate; it is certainly true that anyone driving through a process of change in an organisation such as a prison needs a substantial slice of good fortune. However, it is important to recognise that careful planning can create circumstances in which this luck is more likely to be present. This was the case in Poland at that time. The prison authorities made sure that both staff and prisoners knew why the changes were being introduced and had a reason to support them. This caused the early prisoner unrest to be quickly and peacefully resolved. They made sure that the politicians trusted them in what they were doing and they re-assured the public and the media that there was no threat to public safety.

For a few years during the last decade of the 20th century the Polish prison system shone as a beacon. It was a model of how a decent and humane prison system might operate not only for the countries to its east but also for those in Western Europe. Sadly, as both it and the country in general have been drawn more into the orbit of Western Europe, the prison system has begun to take on many of the less attractive characteristics of its Western European counterparts. Significant increases in the prison population have led to levels of overcrowding reminiscent of the days of the Warsaw Pact. Western models of centralised prison management have all but obliterated the style of regional management partnerships which existed in the 1990s. Most recently the adoption of the Western European habit of identifying allegedly dangerous prisoners and treating them differently from other prisoners has led to an increase in this new group of prisoners.

Russia

Inevitably the country which is the closest inheritor of the traditions of the old Soviet Union is the Russian Federation. It has the third largest number of prisoners in the world after the United States and China, just under one million in total (Walmsley, 2002). However, the most striking feature of recent years has been the fact that government ministers and officials have not attempted to conceal the tragedy of their prison system and have shown a determination to improve matters.

About twenty per cent of all prisoners in Russia are "pre-trial", that is, they have not yet been convicted. Most of them are held in "investigative isolators", known by their Russian acronym, SIZOs. It is there that the worst effects of overcrowding are to be found. A typical accommodation room might be 80 square metres, which would reasonably be expected to hold 20 prisoners. It will in fact contain 40 bunk beds, usually in three tiers, all pushed close together so that the prisoners who sleep on the inner ones have neither light nor ventilation. They are pushed up like this so that maximum use can be made of the remaining available space in the room. To have 40 prisoners living in a room like this would be intolerable. In reality there may be up to 100 men in each room. This means that they have to sleep in three shifts. The most senior or the strongest sleep during the night. Those whose turn to sleep comes during the day will probably forsake the opportunity of one hour's exercise in an outside pen. In the middle of the room there will be a long table with benches on either side, where those prisoners who can find space will take their meals. In the corner will be a hopelessly inadequate toilet, with a single tap to meet everyone's needs for washing and drinking. The whole room will be festooned with lines of drying personal clothing.

In general prisoners are taken out of the room only for interrogation in connection with their cases or for one hour's exercise each day. In addition to security grilles, steel or wooden shutters to prevent prisoners communicating from room to room often cover the windows in the room. The consequence is that natural light and fresh air are virtually excluded. During the winter these rooms become iceboxes, in summer they are baking cauldrons, especially in prisons located in the middle of the Russian landmass. Environments such as this are inevitably breeding grounds for infectious diseases. The Russian authorities themselves estimate that about ten per cent of all prisoners have active tuberculosis, many of them having contracted this while being held in custody as a direct result of their living conditions. The International Centre for Prison Studies has published a commentary on the consequences of this scourge of TB for both the prison system and for the rest of civil society. The title of this book, "Sentenced to Die?" is a quotation from the director of a special anti-tuberculosis prison colony in Russia who commented that the sentence of imprisonment imposed by the court became a death sentence once prisoners contracted tuberculosis (Stern, 1999b).

In common with other countries in the Council of Europe the Russian Federation has a de facto abolition of the death penalty. One consequence of this has been the creation of a new class of life sentence prisoners. They face the prospect of serving at least 25 years in prison, the first ten of those in either solitary or small group confinement. In terms of developing a decent form of management of this new group of prisoners, the hands of the prison administration have been tied since the law stipulates the conditions in which these prisoners have to be held. As a result, the prison authorities are developing plans to create special prison colonies for life sentence prisoners despite evidence from elsewhere about the advantages of keeping life sentence prisoners with others who are serving long sentences.

These are just a few of the challenges that would weaken the enthusiasm of the most committed prison manager. Yet, among those at the top of the Russian Ministry of Justice and of the national prison administration (GUIN), there is a determination to achieve change which should humble the outside experts from agencies such as the Council of Europe who come to Russia with advice about how to reform its prison system. The extent to which the Russian government is prepared to listen to those who come from prison systems in Western European countries, which have achieved much less in the way of reform despite having many more resources, is a lesson to others. The Russian authorities still have a long road to travel; their determination to do so should inspire prison managers in other countries.

Ukraine

The prisons of Ukraine suffer from many of the same problems as those in Russia. They can be summed up as overcrowding, lack of resources, poor training of staff, lack of activity for prisoners and poor health of prisoners, particularly in respect of infectious diseases. Despite the efforts of some committed individuals within the prison system, Ukraine has been slow to begin a realistic process of prison reform. The main reason for this has been the absence of a will at a political and senior administrative level to introduce meaningful change.

One example of this was the response of the government to the strong recommendation which the Council of Europe makes to all new accession states that responsibility for the administration of the prison system should be transferred from the Ministry of the Interior to the Ministry of Justice. The majority of such states, including Russia, have implemented this change. There was strong reluctance in Ukraine to do so, not least because of an understandable fear that the conditions of employment for staff would suffer. Uniformed staff in the Ministry of the Interior are entitled to a number of advantages, including free travel, medical care, subsidised accommodation and holidays. These are important considerations for staff who have low rates of pay. In most other countries these issues were taken on board as part of the transfer arrangements between the two ministries. These matters are referred to more extensively in the following chapter.

In Ukraine it was decided that instead of transferring responsibility for prison administration to the Ministry of Justice a new State Department for the Execution of Punishments would be set up. In addition to the administrative consequences, this new arrangement passed a powerful message that there was at that time no real intention at the most senior level to implement radical reform. This message was heard and understood at lower levels and has meant that in strategic terms the prison system in Ukraine has hardly begun the process of reform. At the same time it has to be recognised that there has been a significant reduction in the overall prison population and in certain areas, where there is local enthusiasm for change, progress has been made.

Kazakhstan

With a prison population of 84,000 in April 2001 (Walmsley, 2002) and a national population of 16 million, Kazakhstan has one of the highest ratios of prisoners to population in the world. This is due in part to its legacy as one of the centres of the Soviet gulag, to which prisoners from all over the Soviet Union were sent. Since the beginning of 1998 the prison administration has been involved in a far-reaching agenda of penal reform. In addition to internal initiatives there has been co-operation with international agencies and non-governmental organisations in a major programme of prison reform and legislative change which will allow the introduction of alternatives to imprisonment. There have been several significant features of the prison reform programme.

No prison system can be reformed in a vacuum. Reform has to be linked to developments in other parts of the criminal justice system. This process began in Kazakhstan with important changes in legislation. There also has to be a recognition that prisons exists to serve their communities. First tentative steps to involve local communities with the process of penal reform have taken place with the introduction of monitoring committees in some regions.

As in other prison systems in the region, one of the major problems within the prison system in Kazakhstan is the high incidence of tuberculosis. This problem initially came to public attention when prisoners with active tuberculosis began to be released into the community and to infect those with whom they came into contact. An important element of the prison reform programme which began in 1998 in Pawlodar region in the north east of Kazakhstan and which has now been extended to three of the largest regions in the country, has been the close link between the initiatives for prison reform and the management of tuberculosis. The terrible physical conditions which exist in many prisons and colonies are a major contributory factor in the spread of tuberculosis. These include overcrowding, lack of proper light and ventilation and poor diet. The problem of tuberculosis in prisons and colonies will only be reduced and eventually eliminated if the need for prison reform is also recognised. The Ministry of Health in Kazakhstan is now beginning to accept that it will have to work closely with the prison health authorities if this epidemic is to be contained.

Another important element of prison reform in this country has been a recognition that there is not likely to be any major increase in the funding available for the administration of prisons either from internal or external sources. People who have worked in prisons and colonies know that the key to a well-managed prison system lies in the human relationships between staff and prisoners. It is possible to have a decent and humane prison system even if financial and other resources are limited. Equally, a prison system can be brutal and inhumane even though it is well funded and well resourced. So, initiatives for penal reform have concentrated on the need for staff to treat prisoners in a firm but decent manner and for prisoners to respond in a similar manner. Such an approach is the first step to developing a better model for prison management.

Finally, the prison authorities of Kazakhstan have been prepared to work in a genuine partnership with experts from other countries. The main groups of foreign prison experts have come from Poland and the United Kingdom. There has been no suggestion that these experts have all the answers and simply come to pass on their knowledge. On the contrary, the real experts on prisons in Kazakhstan are the prison authorities themselves. The task of the foreign experts has been to work alongside them and to give them the benefit of their international experience. Since 1998 there have been biannual visits to Kazakhstan to develop a set of strategic plans and Kazakh officials have visited Poland and the United Kingdom to observe initiatives for prison reform in those countries. Working together, the prison practitioners have analysed all the international human rights instruments that apply to prisoners and people deprived of their liberty. They have considered how these international instruments should be applied to prisoners in Kazakhstan and have begun to draw up plans for the implementation of these international instruments in the context of practical prison management.

Western Europe

At first glance one might think that the challenges facing the prison administrations in the countries of Western Europe are much less than those of their counterparts in Eastern Europe and Central Asia. Resources, staffing levels and general conditions are usually much better. Although there is overcrowding in many countries, it is less intense. Every prisoner at least has a bed and at worst there will be two prisoners sharing a small room designed for one. Health standards and the general treatment of prisoners are much better than in Eastern

Europe. However, closer examination shows that there is a different but no less complex set of problems to be faced by prison managers in these countries.

Overcrowding

The comparative growth in prison populations in a number of countries in recent years has been very significant. Between 1983 and 2000 in the Netherlands, for example, the rate of imprisonment increased from 28 (Council of Europe, 1983:14) to 90 (Council of Europe, 2001:11). In England and Wales there were 76 per cent more people in prison in August 2002 than there were in December 1992 (Prison Service website www.hmprisonservice.gov.uk and Prison Service 1992:1). The number of women in prison has more than doubled since 1986 (Home Office, 2001:3).

In most of the countries involved, this rise in the prison population has not been linked to any obvious increase in crime rates or detection rates. It has largely been a matter of judges sending an increasing proportion of offenders to prison for longer periods. In other words, courts have been making greater use of imprisonment as a punishment.[2]

Inevitably overcrowding has consequences for the prisoners involved, for the staff who look after them and for the entire prison system. In many prison systems overcrowding is unevenly spread. Even when the statistics show that there is no overcrowding in total terms, groups of prisoners may be living in significantly overcrowded accommodation. In both Western Europe as well as Eastern Europe this is especially true for pre-trial and remand prisoners.

One measure of overcrowding is the amount of living space for each prisoner. The European Committee for the Prevention of Torture and Inhuman or Degrading Treatment or Punishment (CPT) has recommended 4 square metres per person as a useful measure when trying to improve on wholly unacceptable levels of overcrowding. However in some of its reports it has described an individual cell measuring 4.5 square metres as 'very small', and unsuitable for periods of detention exceeding one or two days, one of 6 square metres as 'rather small', and one of 10 square metres as 'of a good size for individual occupation' but 'rather small' for dual occupation. Cells for individual occupation measuring 8 square metres and 9 square metres have been considered to provide 'entirely satisfactory' and 'reasonable' conditions of detention' (Council of Europe, 1998, 1999b and 1999c).

There are a number of other factors to be considered when defining whether a prison is overcrowded. For example, the amount of time each day that prisoners have to spend in an overcrowded cell or dormitory is relevant. The consequences of overcrowding are worse if prisoners have to spend 23 hours each day in a space of 3 square metres than if they are only confined to that space for sleeping and spend the rest of time in an exercise yard, a workshop or another area of the prison. Overcrowded living conditions are made worse where there is scarcely any natural light and limited ventilation. Also relevant is whether cooking, washing, clothes drying and bathing are all carried out in the cell or whether there are outside facilities for these activities. Overcrowding may also mean that the kitchen facilities are insufficient to produce the required number of meals and that the infrastructure for water, heating and disposal of waste cannot cope.

The CPT has made clear that it regards overcrowding to be an important factor when it comes to consider findings of inhuman or degrading treatment of prisoners:

> Prison overcrowding is an issue of direct relevance to the CPT's mandate. An overcrowded prison entails cramped and unhygienic accommodation; a constant lack of privacy (even when performing such basic tasks as using a sanitary facility); reduced out-of-cell activities, due to excessive workload for the staff and inadequacy of facilities available; overburdened health-care services; conditions conducive to the spreading of transmittable diseases; increased tension and hence more violence between prisoners and between prisoners and staff. This list is far from exhaustive. It is a fundamental requirement that those committed to prison by the courts be held in safe and decent conditions. For so long as overcrowding persists, the risk of prisoners being held in inhuman and degrading conditions of detention will remain.

CPT visit to Hungary, 1999

Management of prisoners serving long sentences

The increasing length of sentences being imposed by courts in a number of countries has led to significant concern about how to manage the growing number of prisoners serving long sentences. In the minds of the public and of politicians, any prisoner serving a long sentence is often automatically assumed to be dangerous, a threat to the public and as such, has to be held in conditions of maximum security.

In the mid-1990s there were two separate high profile multiple escapes from English prisons. These attracted a great deal of media interest and ultimately led to the dismissal of the then Director General of the Prison Service (Lewis, 1997). As a result, supervision arrangements for all long-term prisoners in the system were tightened. Internal movement inside prisons was reduced. Visiting arrangements were severely restricted. In the case of maximum-security prisoners this meant that they were no longer to be allowed any direct physical contacts, even with the closest members of their families. During all visits they were separated from the visitors by thickened glass.

In the early 1990s in the Netherlands there were a number of escapes by high security prisoners. The consequences for the Netherlands Correctional Agency were severe. Security throughout the whole system was increased and a very restricted regime was introduced for high security prisoners. This was reflected in the report published by the CPT following its visit to the Netherlands in 1997 which criticised the Dutch authorities for their treatment of these prisoners (Council of Europe, 1998). The CPT was especially concerned that the authorities refused to remove handcuffs from one prisoner during an interview by CPT members and as a result, this prisoner was not interviewed. The Dutch government was not used to such criticism and provided a very formal response to the comments (Council of Europe, 1999a).

In many countries, prisoners serving long sentences are held in prisons which have been specially built in remote locations. One consequence of this is that staff who are recruited locally come from a different cultural background from many of the prisoners, who are often from urban communities. This frequently creates a tension and mistrust between staff and prisoners. Kumla high security prison in Sweden is a good example of what can happen in such circumstances.[3] The prisoners there, like many city dwellers the world over, tended to regard staff with a rural background as being less sophisticated, and had an undue resentment at being instructed by them. In similar vein, some staff regarded the prisoners as being too smart for their own good and needing to be brought down to size. The majority of the staff, who were recruited when the prison opened, had no previous knowledge or experience of working with prisoners, certainly not those of the high security category to be held in Kumla. They were fearful that what they were being asked to do would put them at risk when dealing with what they perceived as dangerous and threatening individuals. It should, therefore, have been no surprise that they developed a tradition of dealing reasonably well with security matters while avoiding all close personal contact with prisoners. The consequences of this attitude on the part of the staff quickly became apparent. Within a short period of time Kumla was seen as different from other prisons in Sweden by both staff and prisoners. The behaviour of prisoners changed for the worse when they arrived at Kumla and they began to react in the manner that was expected of them by staff. This is a phenomenon that is not peculiar to Kumla. Many prison systems have one prison that is regarded as being 'the end of the line'. Being sent there is regarded as a badge of honour or of terror for prisoners and often for staff. In the past these would have been prisons such as Dartmoor Prison in England, Marion Penitentiary in the United States and the White Swan Colony in Russia.

When considering how prisoners serving long sentences should be managed, one is inevitably drawn towards consideration of the extent to which such prisoners are more dangerous than other prisoners. The automatic assumption that all long-term prisoners are dangerous is not supported by evidence. Life sentence prisoners, for example, do not in general present more disciplinary problems than any other group of prisoners. On the contrary, they often have better disciplinary records than prisoners serving much shorter sentences. There is no evidence that these prisoners are likely to be more disruptive or to pose a threat to good management merely because of the length of their sentences. Frequently, life sentence prisoners are older than the average age of the convicted prison population. They are often first time offenders who have never previously committed violent acts. Typically, their victim will have been someone they have known previously. Since the final date of release for long-term prisoners will often, at least in part, depend on how they respond in prison, they have an interest in not causing trouble of any kind.

At the same time, a small percentage of long term and life sentence prisoners may well be highly dangerous. Some of them will have committed horrendous crimes and would pose a real threat to the safety of the public if they were to escape. It is the responsibility of prison administrations to make sure that prisoners like this do not escape and also that they do not present a threat to the safety of staff and other prisoners. Managing these prisoners in a manner which is decent and humane while at the same time ensuring the safety of other people is a great challenge to professional prison management.

Political expectations

Democracy survives and is strengthened in a climate where there is vibrant debate about issues which affect the daily lives of citizens, such as health, education, employment, housing, transport and taxation. In a number of countries this debate has now been extended into the role of imprisonment, what it should involve and the extent to which it can contribute to the safety of society.

In some countries in recent years, for example, there has been an increasing political expectation that prisons can make an important contribution to crime reduction strategies by requiring individual prisoners to undertake specific programmes and courses while in prison in the expectation that this will lead them to break away from criminal activities after they are released. In the United Kingdom, for example, the government has been especially demanding about predictions of recidivism when considering prisoners for early release on parole or licence. Prisoners are now expected to undertake a variety of courses, called "programmes", which attempt to change the behaviour which led to them committing crimes and they are not considered for early or conditional release until they have done so. Many practitioners and academics are very doubtful as to whether achieving a reduction in re-offending rates can ever be a direct objective for a prison system. It is true that one task of prison management for many years has been to use the time that men and women are in prison to provide them with skills which will increase the possibility that they will find work on release, to help them to find accommodation on release and to set up support mechanisms which they can use in the community. It is right that they should now be expected to carry out these tasks in a more professional and organised manner than has been done in the past. One might also hope that individually targetted plans to encourage prisoners to change their behaviour and to provide them with skills and the abilities to live as law abiding citizens might prove successful in some cases. However, the suggestion that the prison itself can make a direct contribution to a reduction of crime in civil society is yet to be proved. In England and Wales, for example, only 0.3% of all offences committed result in someone receiving a prison sentence (Home Office, 1999). In view of this figure, it is hard to see how even the most successful prison programmes can have other than a marginal effect on overall crime rates. Yet that is a target which is being set for prison management in some countries. This approach contrasts with that in other European countries where prison authorities give a much higher priority to re-integrating prisoners into their communities by making sure that they have accommodation to return to, employment to take up and some form of personal and social support system.

In the course of the cultural change project the steering group was given examples in a number of countries where the expectations of politicians and other public commentators about the role of the prison were influencing the style and content of management within prison administrations.

Prisons reflect some of the major issues in society

Prisons do not exist in isolation from the rest of society, rather they often reflect its deepest dilemmas; dilemmas which have to be tackled daily by those in charge of the prisons. Nowhere in Europe is this more obvious than in Turkey. For many years the Turkish state has been challenged by significant minority groups which do not accept the political situation. In response the government has introduced extensive anti-terrorist legislation. One consequence of this is that out of 61,000 prisoners, about 11,000 have been convicted or are being held under the anti-terrorist legislation. Included among this number are some that have been convicted of the most horrific crimes, along with others who have committed what would in other countries be regarded as acts of legitimate political protest. These prisoners have considerable group solidarity and there is tremendous peer pressure among them not to conform in any way to the demands of the system, legitimate or otherwise.

This situation has had terrible consequences for the way in which prisons are managed. Many of the 50,000 'ordinary' prisoners are held in district prisons which are as well run as many elsewhere in Europe. However, all the political, media and international interest is focussed on those who are held in a relatively small number of prisons under the anti-terrorist legislation. The way that these prisoners are managed is determined by political and other considerations which, are to a great extent, beyond the control of prison managers.

Although Turkey is an extreme example of this situation, it is not unique. Until recently the work of the Northern Ireland Prison Service was influenced strongly by the political situation in which it operated and a number of other prison administrations, such as Spain, face similar problems on a smaller scale.

United States of America

Between 1980 and 2001 the number of individuals in the jails and prisons of the United States increased almost fourfold. In 1980 the figure was 501,886. This number had reached more than one million by 1990 and by 1995 was over 1.5 million (US Bureau of Justice, 1995:2). By the end of 2001 there were nearly two million men, women and children imprisoned in the USA (US Bureau of Justice, 2002:2).

At a rate of 700 per 100,000 of the total population this is the highest known rate of imprisonment in the world (Walmsley, 2002) with the exception of Rwanda, where there are unique circumstances. With just under five per cent of the world's total population (McDevitt and Rowe, 2002) the United States has 23 per cent of the world's prisoners (Walmsley, 2001). In the States of Louisiana and Texas and the District of Columbia over one per cent of the entire population is in prison or jail custody, according to statistics collated by the International Centre for Prison Studies for its *World Prison Brief Online* (World Prison Brief 2002).

These are figures which set the United States apart from the rest of the democratic world and which are a constant source of wonder for public commentators, prison professionals and researchers in other countries. Why should it be necessary in the 'land of the free' to deprive so many citizens of their liberty? Who are these two million men, women and children? What happens to them while they are in custody? What happens to them after they are released? These are important questions but they go far beyond the scope of this volume.

These prisoners are held in a variety of different kinds of prisons. Those awaiting trial on minor offences or serving short sentences are usually held in local jails, which are managed by local police departments. Those charged or sentenced by state courts are held in prisons managed by individual state Departments of Corrections. Those detained under federal law are held by the Federal Bureau of Prisons. The consequences of the tremendous increase in prison and jail numbers has been felt at all of these levels and the response by prison administrations has been varied. In some cases, as in so many other countries, prisons have simply become more overcrowded with the inevitable consequent pressures on living space, cooking, hygiene and medical provision and an increasing likelihood of violence (Chesney-Lind, 1998). It has become common to house prisoners in sports halls and education units (Monterey County, 2000). In some parts of the country authorities have resorted to holding prisoners in tents (US Department of Justice, 1997).

There has been another unintended consequence of the rise in the numbers of prisoners throughout the United States. Traditionally communities have been reluctant to have prisons in their midst. In many rural and industrially depressed parts of the United States communities are now vying with each other to offer preferential terms for the construction of new prisons, which they see as a way of bringing a much needed boost to local economies. On occasion this has even involved the construction of prisons where there is no local need, either in the anticipation of a future rise in prisoner numbers or, more bizarrely, with the intention of enticing states which have overcrowding to rent the available accommodation. In some cases this trawling for business has proved successful; in September 2000 1,100 of the 3,800 prisoners held by the State of Hawaii were located "out of state" (Matsunaga, 2000). Given the geographical location of Hawaii this inevitably meant that many of them were thousands of kilometres from home; an experience which was disorienting for the prisoners and made it virtually impossible for their families to visit them. This wider economic twist to imprisonment has also been influenced by the involvement of the commercial companies which specialise in the "prison business". This matter is referred to in chapter four.

These factors have all had a significant impact on the way prisons and jails are managed in the United States. Other major considerations include the gross racial disparities, with 62 per cent of all prisoners being Black American or Hispanic (Sentencing Project, 2002). In some states prison management also has to cope with the implications of the continuing use of capital punishment. Another peculiarity of imprisonment in the United States is the relatively high number of prisoners who are held in maximum-security conditions, which amount to individual or group solitary confinement. At the end of 1998 1.8% of all prisoners serving one year or more in state and federal prisons were held in what is colloquially described as "supermax" conditions. This figure is far in excess of figures in comparative jurisdictions; in England and Wales, for example, it is 0.1% (King, 1999).

One of the features which distinguishes prison management in the United States from that in many other countries is the extent to which the use of imprisonment has become an issue of great political, media and public interest. This means that prison and jail managers frequently have to carry out their professional duties under intense media scrutiny.

Latin America

The one word which characterises many of the prison systems in Latin America is violence: violence of prisoner against prisoner, prisoner against staff and staff against prisoner. It is quite common, particularly in large urban prisons, that staff do not enter the areas in which prisoners are accommodated unless they have an armed escort.

> As we went through the internal security gates we were joined by our escort of about 20 baton carrying guards, two of whom were carrying guns with what appeared to be tear gas canisters and one of whom had a pistol.
>
> **Report of an ICPS visit to a prison in Colombia.**

This is especially true in the countries where the main accommodation for male prisoners is in large complexes known as patios. These usually consist of blocks of cells up to four stories high overlooking an internal patio. The ground floor will often be given over to a series of rooms for common use, including a laundry and washing area, a canteen or shop and rooms for arts and crafts, music or a library. In the larger prisons each patio may hold up to 600 prisoners. Each patio will have a self-appointed leader, who will always be surrounded by his team of supporters.

Staff will unlock the rooms early in the morning. Until the evening prisoners have free movement around the patio. Except that the movement is anything but free. Access to the common rooms will be strictly controlled by the lead prisoners and will be restricted to those who can pay. The same will apply to all other facilities. In the worst prisons prisoners have to pay to get food and even to be allocated a bed for sleeping. Prisoners who have no money or patronage from the stronger prisoners will be subject to physical and sexual abuse.

It is common practice to allow families and friends to visit at weekends. The visiting system is very simple: the visitors are allowed into the patios where they move around freely with prisoners. In effect this means that the Sunday visits are conjugal. Frequently there is little check about the relationship between the visitors and the prisoners.

Alternatives to the patio style prisons are those which have pavilions, externally similar to prison accommodation blocks the world over. A typical block might consist of three storied units of large rooms leading off a central corridor. Each large room will be sub-divided by the prisoners themselves with a maze of hanging cloths. The strongest prisoners will have sole possession of one of the sub-divisions; the weakest will have to share with many others. The majority of beds will be made of wooden pallets since the prisoners break up normal steel beds to make weapons. Prisoners are allocated and live according to their financial and social status. The whole atmosphere is likely to be dark, dank and unhealthy.

In one such prison in Venezuela prisoners never come in contact with those from other units because of gang warfare. The grilles at the entrance to each unit are padlocked with two chains. One is controlled by staff from the outside, the other by the prisoners from the inside. This is to prevent any attempt by prisoners from another gang to enter. Prisoners take it in turn throughout the night to sit on guard on a small stool at this grille in 3-hour shifts. His own peers will kill any prisoner who falls asleep during this duty.

> Toilets consisted of a row of open holes with no privacy. Each was stinking and filthy. Large rats were running around without any fear. Behind the toilet area was an equally dirty shower area. At the end of the toilet area rubbish was lying about a metre deep. The director told us that prisoners deliberately keep the area dirty so that they can hide guns and other weapons inside it. In the course of our visit he regularly pointed out areas which were used to hide guns or mobile telephones. Numbers of prisoners followed us everywhere and he spoke quite openly about this in front of them.
>
> **Report of an ICPS visit to a prison in Venezuela.**

It is not uncommon for large prisons to have only four or five guards on duty at any one time. They never enter the patios or pavilions without an armed escort. External perimeter security for the prisons is often in the hands of the national guard rather than prison staff. In the event of a major disturbance they will be called in to restore order, often in an extremely violent manner. In such an environment violence among the prisoners is endemic and there are frequent murders.

The underlying problem is the lack of any political or public interest in prisons and what goes on in them. It is accepted that they are places of violence and chaos. Usually the violence is prisoner on prisoner but in the event that this gets out of hand it is accepted that the National Guard will go in with batons, and sometimes guns, at the ready. In the large inner city prisons never a week goes past without a number of violent deaths. The public long ago ceased to be shocked by this. The lack of government commitment to reform, often exacerbated by political instability, means that with one or two exceptions, it is impossible in many countries to recruit qualified or committed individuals to work within the prison system, either at managerial or at guard level. In some countries young men are able to join the prison system as an alternative to national service in the armed forces and many of them leave as soon as their year's national service has been completed. This means that almost the entire staff can change within a two or three year period.

In many countries staff are given very little training, salary levels are very low and payment may be irregular. In circumstances such as this it is little surprise that corruption is widespread. Everything and everyone has his or her price. Staff who have families to feed and who cannot be sure when their next pay cheque will arrive are easily tempted by well connected prisoners who are willing to pay for weapons and drugs to be brought into prison or for goods to be taken out. In some prisons the corruption is institutionalised and prisoners are required to pay for the use of a bed, for clothing and even for food.

In addition to problems with the recruitment, training and retention of junior prison staff, one of the major barriers to lasting prison reform is the fact that many of the senior staff have little or no experience of the demands of prison management. In a number of countries they are appointed directly by the political head of the relevant ministry and their tenure of office is accordingly directly linked to that person's term of office. This means that even if they do wish to begin a programme of change they will have a very limited time period in which to achieve anything.

There are, however, a number of optimistic signs for the future as some governments have begun to face up to the problems extant within their prison administrations. In Chile, for example, a wide-ranging initiative is underway to develop a new strategy for criminal justice in the country. As part of this initiative the Gendarmería de Chile has begun a major project to introduce strategic planning into its management cycle. This incorporates good operational practice and an understanding of international human rights standards. The Ministry of Justice in Venezuela has also made the first steps towards much needed reform.

In many jurisdictions in Latin America a commitment at political level to effect change is what is initially needed for lasting penal reform. This must be followed by a willingness to appoint and then to support senior officials who are capable of bringing about change. Finally the senior officials must be given the necessary skills to implement this change. In such a context there has to be an understanding that prison management is a highly complex undertaking, which requires careful selection and training of those who are to undertake this task.

Developing countries

The prison as it exists today is a relatively modern construct of western criminal justice systems. Over the last two centuries it has spread around the world as a result of colonial expansion and is now to be found in virtually every country, including quite a number in the developing world, which have no indigenous concept of imprisonment in their cultures. In many countries in sub-Saharan Africa and South Asia for example, prisons are housed in buildings which are well over one hundred years old. These prisons are a legacy from former colonial times, British, French or Portuguese. It is quite disconcerting to be in a town that is otherwise quite African in character and to turn a corner to be confronted by a grandiose building which is a minor replica of a prison in a major European city. Prisons such as this are totally unsuited to the local culture. They were originally built, not to protect local people, but as a means for the colonial power to control local people.

In countries of the developed world prison systems can be a significant drain on public resources and sometimes difficult choices have to be made about providing sufficient resources at the expense of other essential services. In developing countries where resources are scarce the choices are even starker. Most prisoners are young men, who should normally be contributing economically and socially to the good of society. In many cultures the concept of locking up large numbers of them, in a way which makes them unproductive and unable to support their families and which places the burden of their upkeep on the state, makes little economic or cultural sense.

Economic poverty makes it inevitable that the physical conditions of many of these prisons are extremely poor. Prisoners frequently have to sleep on the floor with only a thin blanket between their bodies and the concrete or mud floors. The

Civil Liberties Organisation (1996) in Nigeria has described the reality of this in graphic detail:

> We have three batches in my cell, and I am in Number Two. Other cells have four, even five, when there are many prisoners. When it is time to sleep, we all make space for the first batch. We stand at one end of the cell, or sit. Some of us sleep while standing, but you do not lie down. Only the first batch lies down. After four hours, they get up, and we lie down to sleep. After four hours, we get up, and the third batch will sleep.

In some countries the physical security of the prisons is very poor with low perimeter walls and buildings which have insecure locks or even none at all. To compensate for this, groups of prisoners are kept shackled to a long iron bar, which runs the length of the room in which they are kept. Frequently the prison administration is not able to provide clothing for prisoners. This may mean that years after admission prisoners are wearing clothes which they wore at the start of their imprisonment and which have turned into rags. In many prisons it is impossible for the authorities to feed prisoners adequately.[4] Where it is practicable prisoners depend on their families to provide for their basic needs. More often than not this does not happen, either because the prisoners are held far from their homes or because they have no families. In that case they depend on support from other prisoners or non-governmental organisations, where they exist.

An immediate consequence of all of these circumstances is that the health of prisoners suffers dramatically. In addition to general illness caused by inadequate diet there are specific diseases, such as tuberculosis, which are either brought on or exacerbated by the overcrowded and unhealthy conditions. In the prison systems in a number of countries HIV and AIDS are an increasing scourge.

In many developing countries there is a general lack of access to justice and the consequences of this are felt directly within prison systems. In a number of developing countries 80 per cent of those in prison are awaiting trial (DFID, 2000). It is not uncommon in these circumstances for prisoners to be in prisons waiting to come to trial for longer periods than they would be sentenced to if found guilty. Sometimes delays are caused by a failure of the court process. In other cases it may simply be that neither the prison nor the police authorities have transport to convey the prisoner many kilometres to appear in court.

It is sometimes argued that in countries where resources are scarce for everyone, where law-abiding citizens are starving, have poor accommodation and a lack of proper health care, there can be little justification in devoting resources to improve conditions for prisoners. Such an argument further complicates the already impossible task facing prison managers in these countries who attempt to provide decent and humane conditions for those whom society has decided to deprive of their liberty.

Conclusion

This chapter has described some of the complexities of prison management in different countries. The detailed challenges vary from country to country. In the largest prisons in the world prison directors do their best to manage institutions which hold up to 10,000 people in grossly overcrowded and often-unhealthy conditions. In many prisons in Latin America the main threat to good governance is posed by the all-pervading power of the gang leaders who orchestrate and control violence between prisoners and against staff. Similar problems face many prison wardens in large prisons in the United States. The problems facing prison directors in sub-Saharan Africa, where overcrowding can mean the inability of prisoners to find a place to lie down and where there is widespread hunger and malnutrition, are different from those of the director of a minimum security prison in Western Europe, who has less than one hundred prisoners in his or her care and whose main concern is the need to re-assure local community representatives that the prisoners who go out from the prison each day to work do not threaten their safety.

Despite all these differences, there are common features in the management of such diverse prisons. Underlying all of these is the fact that, despite its high walls and fences, the prison is not an isolated institution. It is a part of civil society and its management is an important element of public service. The following chapter will examine some of the consequences of this.

1   Personal communication from the Polish prison administration to the author.

2   For England and Wales, as an example, see Home Office, 1999

3   Kumla prison, in the County of Örebro, was visited by the project steering group at the invitation of Bertel Österdahl, Director General of the Swedish Prison and Probation Service.

4   See, for example, the Human Rights Watch website at www.hrw.org/prisons/africa

3. Prison management as a public service

Public perceptions

One of the first lessons to be learned by those who are responsible for the management of prisons, at national, regional and individual level, is that they do not work in an isolated environment. The decisions that they take and the manner in which prisons are managed are of great interest to many people far beyond the narrow confines of the prison. For instance, they are likely to be of interest to the media, who are always on the look out for a story. It is a cliché that good news does not sell newspapers and so the stories which are most likely to interest the media will be about things that have gone wrong, such as escapes, riots or other major incidents.

As far as the vast majority of the public is concerned, prisons are a closed, unknown world and this secretiveness increases their fascination. As far as the media is concerned, their main interest in prisons is as a means of feeding this public fascination. This can have important consequences. For example, a prison director can spend a whole lifetime managing prisons well and effectively and never attract more than a few columns of press coverage. Yet one major escape will bring that person immediately to national attention and be the one feature of his or her career for which he or she is remembered.

In some countries a news editor who is short of a story to print can always fill several columns with a report about conditions in a local prison. Depending on the nature of the readership of the newspaper, the story may refer to the prison as a holiday camp, where prisoners are given better accommodation than law-abiding citizens and are able to enjoy many luxuries. Or it may go the other extreme and describe prison as a concentration camp, where brutal guards continually repress prisoners and deprive them of basic human rights. At one level, such superficial considerations can be dismissed as being of no great significance. At another level, they are very important since the perception which the public has of how prisons are run is immediately influenced by what they read in newspapers, hear on the radio or see on television.

Prisons can be seen as coming at the end of the spectrum of the criminal justice process. A spectrum which stretches from the commission of a crime, its investigation, the apprehension of a suspect, a court process, a finding of guilt and finally the passing of a sentence. In that sense prison can be seen as the outcome or final result of criminal justice activities. Once a person has been sentenced to prison the public in general has little interest in what then happens to him or her. Interest in prisons is only aroused when something goes wrong and there is a riot or an escape. In that respect, the success of the prison is often measured in the eyes of the public by the absence of failure. A prison is being successfully managed when there are no escapes and no riots.

This has an immediate consequence for senior prison administrators since they are generally responsible, directly or indirectly, to a government minister. In democratic countries this person will be an elected politician and politicians are usually very sensitive to public opinion. They do not welcome bad publicity about prisons as this may lead to difficulties with their electors.

For these and other reasons prison administrators have to be conscious that their work will often attract public attention. The way that prisons are managed is influenced by wider considerations of public policy, and prison management can be seen as an important measure of the standards expected in public service. This is most obvious in countries which are in transition from totalitarianism to democracy. In many of them, one of the first programmes of reform instituted by a newly elected government is in the penal system. In such circumstances reform of the prison system is seen as a recognition of the importance of universal access to justice in a new democracy. Within that context a reformed prison service carries great symbolism because of the statement it makes about the manner in which citizens may be deprived of their liberty.

The Wider Context

A total of 111 countries have abolished the death penalty in law or practice. Of the 84 countries which retain the death penalty, only a small number actually carry out executions (Amnesty International 2002). This means that in most countries imprisonment is the most severe form of punishment available to the courts.

For this reason it is essential that the way imprisonment is carried out should be subject to public oversight and that politicians, as the elected representatives of civil society, should define the broad context within which prisons are managed. This also means that in trying to identify the key features of cultural and organisational change one has to be aware of these influences. It has been suggested by a number of significant world figures, including Mandela, Churchill and Dostoyevsky, that prison systems can be seen as a reflection of the democratic values of a country (Mandela, 1994, Home Office, 1910:1354 and Dostoyevsky, 1866). The positive consequence of this can be seen in a country such as Poland, which, as it emerged from the traumatic events of 1989, was keen to show that it embraced democratic values. The importance of these values to Polish society at this time was reflected in the way the prison system changed from a coercive organisation to one which tried to reflect values of humanity, decency and respect for all citizens, even those who had been deprived of their liberty.

There is another aspect to this public interest, which has become increasingly important in recent years in a number of the countries under analysis in this study. This is the notion that the prison has a central role to play in protecting citizens by removing from society those people who pose a threat to law-abiding citizens. In a number of European countries there is now a concern, which in some instances amounts almost to an obsession, with public safety and the need to reduce or even to eliminate crime. Governments respond to this with an increasing number of initiatives to prevent crime and to deal with those who are responsible for it. Some of those, who spoke to the steering group which carried out the field work leading to this book, questioned the extent to which it is proper or even practicable to use the criminal justice system to deal with what are often fundamental problems for society. One person expressed this to the group in terms that Europe is now witnessing a return to the control society, which had been abolished in 1945. A more moderate expression of the same concern might be that in many countries political processes are becoming more interventionist. It was suggested that one lesson which Eastern Europe might take from the West is that governments should not promise too much in this extremely complex field.

In relative terms one certainly has to recognise that prison systems operate within different environments in each country. In Poland, for example, the whole concept of prison reform over the last ten or twelve years has to be considered within the context of the wider political environment, as was discussed in chapter two. The prison administrations in England & Wales, the Netherlands and Scotland in recent years have had to cope with unusually close political interest at ministerial level in comparatively low level administrative matters. This has been coupled with and perhaps caused by a high level of public interest in matters of operational detail. This has not been the case in Sweden. Instead, a major consideration for senior management there has been the fact that decisions about dismissal or even transfer of staff are subject to very stringent labour laws which protect the rights of individual members of staff, sometimes at the expense of the good of the organisation. This has frustrated the desire of senior prison management to promote junior staff who had potential and to replace other staff who were unwilling to adopt a new style of working.

It is also true that prison systems are likely to be influenced by the general management structures and styles that are prevalent in a particular country. If civil society at large has little concern in matters of good government, it will be unlikely that this will be a matter of concern within the prison system. An example of these influences can be seen in England and in the Netherlands, where changes in the style of management in government departments towards what has become known as 'results based management' and the introduction of structures that attempt to provide transparency in the performance of government services, have been reflected in the way the prison system is managed. As a result of these changes, prison staff who previously regarded their work as something of a vocation which set them apart from other public sector workers, are now encouraged to see themselves as simply another group of public workers, working in the same environment as other employees in the government or even in the private sector.

One example of this is the way in which conditions of employment, covering such matters as general working hours and job content in the prison service, now have to be broadly comparable to conditions for workers in other areas. In England & Wales and the Netherlands it has been suggested that the elimination of excessive working hours and overtime for prison staff was the prelude to other changes, and that resistance to change in working methods diminished when staff were encouraged to see themselves within this wider context. An instance of this was seen in countries where staff attitudes began to change considerably when the obligation on them to live in official accommodation provided in the shadow of the prison was removed. Many moved with their families to live beside other members of the community.

As a practical example of the improvement in staff working conditions, in Barlinnie Prison in Scotland the project steering group noted that many of the working conditions and leisure-time facilities such as the staff canteen and fitness-rooms are now as good as in the best private firms. In Poland, on the other hand, the prison service might well be entering a period of risk because of developments in this area. As prison staff have moved away from a military model they have had to forfeit the higher levels of income traditionally paid to those in the uniformed sectors of public service. At the same time, working conditions and salaries in the private sector are increasing as the economy is modernised. As a consequence, the prison service is finding it difficult to recruit good staff and is indeed losing some of those they already have at an accelerating rate. This is compounded by the fact that working conditions in many Polish prisons are not attractive because many of the buildings have changed little since they were built in the nineteenth century.

In common with all other large public institutions, prison systems are influenced in a variety of respects by the environments in which they exist. In general terms, the extent to which a criminal justice system makes use of prison as a punishment may say a great deal about the view which civil society has of itself. An excessive use of imprisonment may indicate that a society is insecure or is punitive; that it wishes to exclude everyone whose behaviour is seen as a threat to what is considered to be the norm. More confident societies may look for court disposals which are less retributive towards the offender, which are more effective in meeting the needs of victims and which are more efficient in contributing to a reduction in levels of crime. The way in which other elements of the criminal justice process operate will affect the way prisons are managed. The prison system in each jurisdiction will also be affected by the general style of management for public institutions As a publicly managed civil institution, the prison administration will be governed by the regulations which apply to all public sector organisations in the country; these may be particularly relevant in respect of the employment, training and salaries of staff. One example of this, as described above, is how employment legislation in Sweden has made it very difficult for senior management to appoint younger, more committed staff in place of staff who are unwilling to change working practices. These and other considerations will, to a greater or lesser extent, influence the development of the prison system in any country.

Public Accountability

Until relatively recently it was possible to describe the prison as the last great secretive institution in democratic society. Once the courts of justice had decreed that criminals should be deprived of liberty, the gates of the prison clanged shut behind them. From that moment on civil society had no further interest in how these men and women were treated or what happened to them. In most jurisdictions this is no longer the case. Given what has been said previously about the increased concern for public safety, there is now an expectation that when prisoners are released they will be less of a threat to the public than they were before they entered prison. In this respect those responsible for the administration of prisons recognise that they have to be accountable to civil society for what happens within prisons.

Public accountability can be expressed in a variety of ways. It starts with a responsibility on the administration to let the public know what happens behind the high walls and fences of its prisons and what civil society is entitled realistically to expect in terms of the outcomes of imprisonment. This may be done formally by having mechanisms for independent oversight and inspection of prisons and prison systems. In some jurisdictions this is achieved through a judicial process; in others, there is an administrative process, such as the independent inspectors of prisons in the United Kingdom. In some countries there are also arrangements for responsible members of the community to ensure that prisons are managed in a decent and humane manner. Informal mechanisms for public accountability are also very important. This is likely to involve encouraging non-governmental organisations and other groupings of public citizens to visit prisons and to take part in some of the activities which go on inside them. In this way the public may begin to have an understanding of which conditions are likely to help prisoners to integrate safely back into society and which, on the other hand, might lead to further recidivism.

In respect of their accountability for public safety, a number of prison administrations are now giving a high priority to what is known as risk assessment. This involves an assessment of each individual prisoner based on a number of factors. As regards the conditions of imprisonment, there will be an assessment of the level of security to which prisoners should be subjected. This will depend on consideration of the possibility that they may attempt to escape and the likelihood that they may have external support for any attempt. There will also be an assessment of the amount of control to which they should be subjected in prison. This will be based on considerations as to whether they are likely to be troublesome or not, whether they can be trusted to obey the regulations of the prison, whether they are likely to be a threat to the physical safety of staff and whether they will present a threat to other prisoners or be liable to be threatened by them.

When considering public accountability in the context of cultural change, it becomes necessary to make staff aware that it is no longer sufficient to regard the person in prison merely as a prisoner. Like all human beings, the person who is in prison has a myriad of personal relationships that affect his or her personal development. In addition to the relationships that are made and broken with other prisoners and with prison staff, there are relationships with family and friends, perhaps with former victims, and relationships within the community to which the prisoner will return on release. Any one of these sets of relationships will have a greater or lesser influence on the prisoner at any one time and prison staff have to be continually aware of this.

Prison staff have no option but to deliver the various objectives set for them by government, particularly when they include attempts to reduce the likelihood that people who are in prison will commit further offences after release. This means that there has to be a greater emphasis on seeing prisoners as individuals rather than as a homogenous group. This is likely to result in a much sharper focus when it comes to delivering the various activities in prisons, which are known as regimes and programmes, in order to identify those who are likely to benefit from them. Since a number of these activities adopt a behaviourist approach, there are also human rights and ethical issues to be considered as regards the extent to which prisoners can be obliged to undertake courses which do not constitute part of the sentence of the court. There are additional concerns about justice when prisoners who refuse to take part in such courses are refused consideration for parole or early release because they have refused. When this happens there has to be an oversight which is independent of the prison administration. In the Netherlands this is achieved by requiring the court to review such cases every two years.

If one accepts the argument that prison systems are influenced by all of the external factors which have just been described one is drawn to a number of important conclusions. The first is that the politicians who have governmental accountability for the manner in which prisons are administered must lay down the broad principles within which the prison system in their country should operate. Having established the broad parameters, they should then allow the prison administrators to get on with the business of translating these principles into a set of operational procedures to be implemented by staff. The politicians should not involve themselves in the daily running of prisons.

The other side of this argument is that senior prison administrators have to understand the reality, particularly in the modern political climate, that government ministers who are accountable to parliament for what happens in the prison system expect to be protected from any unexpected events which may cause them political embarrassment. In a number of prison administrations such as those in England & Wales, the Netherlands and Sweden, the reality is that ministerial involvement in operational matters has generally happened as a result of political embarrassment following high profile escapes or riots.

"The Ministry"

The public accountability of prison administrations is usually expressed through some form of wider government structure. In most European countries the prison system is now administered within the Ministry of Justice. Historically in Central and Eastern European and Central Asian countries the prison system was part of the Ministry of the Interior. The Council of Europe has made it a virtual condition of entry that new member states should transfer responsibility for prison administration from the Ministry of the Interior to the Ministry of Justice. Paradoxically in one of the oldest of the Council of Europe countries, England & Wales, there is no Ministry of Justice and the prison service is an executive agency of the Home Office or Ministry of the Interior.

The argument for transfer to the Justice Ministry is twofold. In the first place, in a number of countries the Ministry of the Interior is closely identified with the police and traditionally pre-trial detention has been regarded as an important part of the process of crime investigation and criminal identification. International human rights standards call for a full-time prison staff with civil service status. The implication of this is that such staff should be separate from the police or other authority that investigates crime and arrests suspects. One way of ensuring this is to locate them in separate ministries. A second reason for this transfer of responsibility is to emphasise that the prison system should be a civilian rather than a military organisation. This matter is dealt with more fully in the succeeding section.

In organisational terms it is important that the prison system should be in the chain of public accountability. In democratic countries this is achieved through government departments, which are responsible to Ministers, who are in turn accountable to parliament. This is meant to ensure that what goes on in prisons and the way that prisoners are treated can be subjected to parliamentary scrutiny. By definition, the administration of the penalty of imprisonment often has to be implemented in conditions that are not open to public scrutiny and it is, therefore, important that there should be clear limits to the power of those who manage it and to the deprivations that it involves. In democracies these limits are set by laws, which are approved by parliament, and policies, which are determined by Ministers. In reality, as described in the previous section, there is a fine balance to be struck between the involvement of elected politicians in matters of general policy and their interference in the daily management of prisons in a way which might suggest that imprisonment itself is a political rather than a judicial matter. This balance has become increasingly difficult to maintain in many countries where issues surrounding imprisonment have become politically contentious.

The balance can be better achieved when public accountability extends, as it does in the Netherlands, beyond the narrow line running from the Minister of Justice to Parliament. There a variety of supervision mechanisms and of inspection agencies are organised by different Ministries, often with the authority to control different aspects of prison and of life in prison. The reports of these bodies are often published. For example, within the Ministry of Justice there is a Central Advisory Board, whose members visit prisons to check that the conditions of imprisonment are in accordance with legal requirements. In addition, each prison has a legally based local committee, which supervises prison conditions and deals with complaints from prisoners. The National Health Care Inspectorate, which is part of the Ministry of Welfare and Health, supervises the state of medical care and of treatment of mentally disturbed prisoners. The Labour Inspectorate, which is part of the Ministry of Social Affairs, controls the working conditions for staff as well as for prisoners working in prison industries. There is an Inspectorate from the Ministry of Welfare and Health that controls the quality and conditions under which food and meals are delivered. The local government controls safety in relation to risks such as that of fire. The independent Court of Audit has legal authority to audit the performance of the State and its associated bodies and in 2000 audited "the design and operation of the integrity policy in prisons". These inspection and audit bodies are all independent of the prison system and can also act as a countervailing influence to any political attempt to introduce changes which might threaten the humane treatment of prisoners. Other jurisdictions have a similar raft of checks and balances.

In most democratic countries there are traditionally a small number of areas that stand above party politics and which attract a broad political consensus. National defence is a good example of this; political parties may argue about one helicopter more or one battleship less but in general terms, whichever party is in power, there will be broad agreement about how best to secure the safety and security of the country from external threat. A similar consensus may apply to specific issues of great national importance in an individual country. Throughout the last thirty years of the twentieth century, for example, there was broad consensus among all the major political parties in the United Kingdom about how to deal with the political situation in Northern Ireland.

In most European countries from the 1950s until recently there was a similar consensus about the circumstances in which citizens should be deprived of their liberty. There was a recognition that imprisonment should be restricted to those who had committed the most serious offences and those who posed a major threat to the safety of others. It was such a serious punishment that courts should only impose it when no other option was available. It was also generally accepted that imprisonment had a very limited role to play in any attempt to reduce crime in society. In a number of countries, including some involved in this project, this political consensus has shifted in recent years. There is now a willingness to see imprisonment as a major "weapon" in the "war against crime". This has resulted in a significant increase in the use of imprisonment, as described in chapter one. It has also seen increased political involvement in the daily management of prisons, as mentioned in the previous section.

In the course of this project the steering group learned of instances, particularly in England & Wales and the Netherlands, where specific incidents in prisons had triggered major ministerial involvement at a detailed level. In both of these countries there is a tension, which is not always constructive, between the desire to separate the working of the prison administration from direct political involvement, and the desire for government ministers to keep a close watch on matters which may be politically sensitive. In both the Netherlands and in England & Wales there has been an attempt to resolve this problem by creating agencies that are organisationally distinct from the parent ministry. At certain levels this has eased some of these tensions but at other levels there has been no real organisational change.

In Sweden, on the other hand, there is a tradition throughout government and the public service of little ministerial involvement in matters of detail. This has allowed the Swedish Prison and Probation Service to be much more proactive about developing its policies. Recent developments in this area in Poland have been of special interest. As described in chapter two, a number of those interviewed in that country as part of this project were clear that it had been possible to drive through many radical changes in the prison system at the end of the 1980s and the beginning of the 1990s only because government ministers were so involved with other matters that they were not aware of the scope of the changes which were being introduced.

The distinction between setting the principles within which a prison system should operate, which is the legitimate role of the Ministry responsible for prisons, and the daily management of prisons, which is the task of the prison administration, can sometimes be difficult to maintain. However, if prisons are to be managed in a professional and consistent manner it is essential that this distinction should be observed.

The prison system as a civilian organisation

Following the lead given by the United Nations (UN, 1977: Rule 46), the Council of Europe has taken the view that it is important to emphasise that prison staff should have civilian rather than military status. Reference was made in the previous section to the fact that the Council's chosen means of achieving this has been to recommend strongly that the administration of prisons in each country should come under the Ministry of Justice rather than the Ministry of the Interior. However, it needs to be realised that simple transfer of responsibility to a Ministry of Justice does not imply that a prison system has been "demilitarised", that is, converted into a civilian system.

As the word implies, demilitarisation involves the dismantling of the military system of prison management but often there is little notion about what should replace it other than a vague concept of "civilianisation". So far, little thought has been given to the new model structure to which countries should aspire, nor to the process by which this is to be achieved.

In many cases transfer to the Ministry of Justice has occurred with little or no change in the various levels in the military structure, or in the hierarchy, ethos and attitudes. In Russia, for example, despite the transfer of the prison system (GUIN) to the Ministry of Justice, the Special Forces of the prison system ("spetznatz") remain closely associated with the Ministry of the Interior and in recent years have fought alongside other Russian troops in Chechnya. Training in many of these countries still involves a considerable amount of traditional military style exercises and practising with a variety of weapons that will never be used in the management of prisons. Reform programmes involving training staff in human rights for prisoners and prison staff have been added to the former training curriculum rather than replacing elements of it.

In some jurisdictions there have been some significant changes in top management following the transfer to the Ministry of Justice. For example, in Romania magistrates became directors of prisons and directors now wear civilian clothes rather then uniform. However, the introduction of magistrates as directors was greeted with some resentment by other prison staff, not least because their salaries were considerably higher than existing prison directors. The replacement of military uniforms was seen as a purely symbolic gesture since it was not accompanied by any changes in salary, rank or conditions of service.

There is frequently a misunderstanding among staff about what is implied by "demilitarisation" and conversion to a civilian structure. The term "civilianisation" is used loosely to describe the alternative to the military structure. There is a perception among many prison staff that this conversion means that they must change from having a professional military role to becoming administrative clerks. There is a lack of understanding that a modern, professional prison service structure is different from a military structure but that it is also different from a civil service administrative bureaucracy. The desired outcome of demilitarisation is a civilian prison service, in which discipline remains important and in which staff could still wear uniforms. There is a need to develop a set of principles and a model structure for such a service which can be understood as something to aim for and be an incentive to change. Staff must be reassured that a move to civilian status will not diminish their standing in the community by making them appear to be less professional.

There are also likely to be important financial considerations as far as individual members of staff are concerned. In many countries in Eastern Europe and Central Asia members of the military have a number of important benefits. For example, they may be entitled to free travel, to receive free meals when they are on duty and to have excellent pension schemes. They and their families are often entitled to free medical care and to have subsidised holidays. All of these benefits applied to prison staff while they had military rank. The loss of these benefits will mean significant loss of income. It is not sufficient to regard these service benefits merely as privileges that can be abolished at no cost, as if they are illegitimate or corrupt. Salary and conditions of employment in any job, in any society, have to be considered as a legitimate package. Any change to this package of employment should involve re-negotiation to ensure that staff are not placed at a personal disadvantage by any change. In most countries of Eastern and Central Europe some form of compromise has been reached which has allowed staff to retain most if not all their former conditions of employment.

Demilitarisation involves not only changing ranks and uniform but also significantly redefining roles of staff within the prison system. For example, prison staff should not be expected to operate alongside police investigators in order to establish the guilt of people who are held in prison awaiting trial. This applies especially to the staff known in Russian as "operativnik". Prison staff should not be expected to perform military or policing duties as auxiliaries to armed services or police services in times of emergencies as they have, or are trained to do, in some Eastern European and Central Asian countries. Prison staff should be appropriately trained to manage disorder inside prisons, but they should be able to do this using specific techniques which are significantly different to those used in wars or civil disturbances.

If the new prison administration is to be genuinely professional, this will have implications for the manner in which staff are recruited and trained and the standards which they are expected to observe in their work. This issue is dealt with further in chapter five.

There has also been a frequent misconception that change from a military structure to a civilian structure would result in a reduction in expenditure. In fact, the contrary may well happen. For example, even though the salary of individuals might not increase, overall salary costs might well increase significantly with civilianisation. In a military structure a member of staff can be ordered to work as many hours as are necessary with no additional payment beyond the basic salary. Thus many prison staff in military structures work very long and unpredictable hours. In a civilian structure, overtime or its equivalent usually has to be paid to staff who work more hours than their contract provides for. There may also have to be an increase in the numbers of staff, not only in order to deal with prisoners in a more humane manner but also, for example, to provide the external perimeter security cover that was previously provided by military conscripts. These financial problems can be compounded by the fact that in many countries Ministries of Justice have fewer resources to draw on than the larger and more powerful Ministries of the Interior.

National, federal and local structures

In the world of modern government, institutional structures are frequently very complex. As a result they are usually organised at different levels. For example, national policy on education will be set by a department of central government but the implementation of that policy will probably be delegated to a regional level. This second tier of authority will often have considerable freedom in the way it delivers services, provided it does so within the broad parameters of national policy. Some countries have a federal system of government, in which there is a clear distinction between matters of national importance such as the economy or defence, which are organised federally and those other services which can be organised within states or provinces.

These are issues that also need to be considered in respect of prison administration. Within some large countries there are a number of discrete prison systems, reflecting the wider political arrangements of the country. The most extreme example of such division is in the United States, which has a federal prison system, fifty state prison systems and hundreds of county and district prison systems. These three tiers are not hierarchical in administrative terms; the Federal Bureau of Prisons has no authority over the state or county systems, although it has in the past attempted to operate to a set of professional standards to which other prison systems might aspire. Offenders are allocated to one of the three systems according to the court that deals with their case. Legislative changes and new government policies relating to issues such as drugs have changed the structure and size of many of these prison systems over the last twenty years. As more criminal acts became covered by federal legislation, the prison population within the Federal Bureau of Prisons quadrupled in the 20 years after 1980, as described in chapter one. A number of state prison systems, such as those of Texas and California, with 162,070 and 159,444 prisoners respectively, became larger than those of most independent countries (US Bureau of Justice Statistics, 2002).

A number of other countries that are governed on a federal basis also operate state prison systems. These include Australia, Brazil, Germany, India, and Switzerland. In some of these, such as Brazil and Germany, there are units within the federal Ministry of Justice which have some responsibility for policy issues relating to prisons, but they generally have little or no authority over the administrative structures in state prison systems. In India, the Bureau of Police Research and Development has tried to introduce training programmes for prison staff, so far with very little success. A similar initiative in Switzerland has been much more successful, which is hardly surprising, given the much smaller organisational scale.

Most countries in the world have prison systems that are organised on a national basis. After China, the largest of these is in the Russian Federation, with almost one thousand prisons, stretching over eleven time zones and holding just under one million prisoners. It would clearly be impossible to organise every detail of prison management at a national level in most large countries, let alone in Russia. Those systems which organise themselves most successfully tend to be ones which have set national parameters to ensure that standards set by international and national legislation will be adhered to and which then allow regional or local management to implement the agreed operating standards in a flexible manner.

Two good examples of this style of management are to be found in the Netherlands and in Sweden. The cluster style of administration, which is being developed in the National Agency for Correctional Institutions in the Netherlands, permits the development of local initiative within nationally agreed boundaries. Most clusters contain pre-trial prisons as well as low and high security prisons. This means that the majority of prisoners can serve their entire sentence within their local cluster. Prisons have built up close links with local welfare, housing and employment agencies as a means of enabling prisoners to settle back into their communities after release. In Sweden the joint management of groups of local prisons and local probation services is intended to foster similar local links. The national Prison and Probation Service has a light touch in ensuring that national standards are met and in setting budgets but is content to allow the senior prison director in the local area to lead the team of managers in implementing national policy according to local needs.

The important feature of this style of management is that it implies a significant degree of trust between the administrators in the national system and local prison managers. In many prison systems this trust does not exist. The first concern of the national administrators is often to ensure that government ministers are not embarrassed by anything that goes wrong within the country's prisons. This was referred to at the beginning of this chapter. The national administrators are very often not confident that local prison directors give sufficient priority to this consideration and, therefore, are reluctant to allow them to exercise too much initiative for fear that things may go wrong. Prison directors become conscious of this and will be aware that it is often more important to make sure that nothing goes wrong rather than that things go right. Such an approach results in a system which aims for minimum standards rather than for maximum delivery.

In a professionally managed prison system the national administrators will encourage local prison directors to use their initiative in implementing national strategies in innovative ways. There will be an expectation that matters will be dealt with effectively and efficiently but also an appreciation that from time to time things will go wrong. Provided the nationally determined guidelines have been followed, a professional system can cope with such failures from time to time. The possibility that they may occur occasionally should not be used as an excuse for insisting on a style of administration that tries to control every operational detail from a national centre.

Part of the public service

If one accepts the principles described in this chapter, one comes to realise that no prison or prison system can exist in a vacuum. In the first place, it cannot be administered without full reference to other departments of government, especially other criminal justice agencies. Secondly, within prisons, activities and programmes to help prisoners to reform themselves cannot be confined to the closed environment of the prison. They must be closely linked to services that are available for all other citizens in the community.

Traditionally, many prison systems have operated in an isolated environment. They have failed to recognise the need to be associated with other government initiatives and they have seen little need to take account of what happens in their local communities. This is no longer acceptable, nor is it a professional way to manage a prison system. The next chapter deals with how prison systems have to react to the changing environment that surrounds them.

4. Prison management in a changing environment

Overview

We have already seen that the prison system in each country is affected to a large degree by the political and social climate in which it exists. Given that prisons exist to serve the public good, this is as it should be. The manner in which a society deprives certain citizens of their liberty has to be subject to strict legal and parliamentary control and should be a matter for public and political debate. These controls and this debate may differ, at least in degree, in individual countries and these differences will have a direct effect on the way that prisons are managed. For example, in most countries of Western Europe and North America there has been a traditional expectation that prison should include some form of treatment for individual prisoners. As a result, prison management has often focussed on creating an ethos within the prison in which it is possible to influence the personalities of individual prisoners and to change their future behaviour. In less individualistic and more communitarian cultures, for example in many countries of sub-Saharan Africa, a behavioural approach like this is neither appropriate nor practical. In many countries of Eastern Europe and Central Asia the collapse of the Soviet model of imprisonment, which consisted of exile and industrial work for the state, has left a vacuum that has not yet been filled.

Prison management needs to take account of the political and cultural environment which surrounds it. This has been particularly true in the climate of radical change which has existed in so many parts of the world over the last twenty years. This implies that good prison management needs to be dynamic rather than static and that any process of improvement has to be a continuous one. A related reason for this is the fact that prison management is primarily not about systems and processes but about people: staff and prisoners.

That is not to say that the process of good prison management is purely situational, depending solely on the legal and political environment of each country. As we shall see shortly, there is an agreed set of international standards, accepted by the vast majority of countries, against which prison management can be assessed. It is also possible to identify a set of parameters within which appropriate models of good prison management can be developed; models that take account of the need for cultural and organisational change.

The history of the organisation

It has already been noted that no large organisation such as a prison system exists in a vacuum. It has not come to be as it is by accident but will have developed incrementally as a result of the environment in which it exists. It carries within it a great deal of institutional history and baggage. In the United Kingdom, for example, the modern prison system can trace its origins to the nineteenth century reforms which placed an emphasis on the need to secure the personal rehabilitation of individual prisoners. At its beginning this owed much to the involvement of Christian reformers. In the twentieth century this notion of personal rehabilitation took on a more secular tone, although it never quite lost its religious undertones. Reference has already been made to the fact that the concept of personal reform is now finding a new quasi-scientific expression through the influence of psychology on attempts to change the behaviour of prisoners by means of various courses and programmes which they are obliged to undertake. This is happening not only in the United Kingdom but also in countries such as Canada and New Zealand. It has been suggested that the reductionist stance on imprisonment adopted in the Netherlands after the Second World War owed much to the experiences of loss of liberty during the war years by people who subsequently became responsible for criminal justice matters in that country. If this was the case, one might wonder to what extent the significant increase in prison numbers in the Netherlands during the last years of the twentieth century can be attributed to the fact that a new generation of politicians and officials came to power during that period. In Poland the traditional style of imprisonment followed that of the Soviet Union in general terms, with imprisonment being largely a method of exile from the community. The process of fundamental change which began in the 1980s as part of an increasing expression of wider radical change within the country has already been described in chapter two. In the words of Pawel Moczydlowski, Director General of the Polish prison system throughout the period of most radical change, "The best opportunity for radical change in a prison system is when there is a revolution in the country".[1]

The first step towards cultural and organisational change in any prison system is an understanding of the roots of that system. In order to establish the direction in which a system should develop, one has to know where it has come from. Given the traditional nature of most prison systems, it is surprising that so many of them have such short institutional memories. Events of comparatively major significance are forgotten relatively quickly, even by those who had been involved in them. This often means that systems do not learn from past successes and failures. Instead there is often a continuous re-inventing of the wheel. This is frequently compounded by poor record keeping which means that those who wish to learn from the past are prevented from doing so. It is essential that anyone who wishes to begin a process of change must have an understanding of the historical baggage that each prison system carries. This is necessary for any new manager who comes from outside the system. It is also important to be aware that it is not safe to assume that every person who works inside a prison system, even over many years, has the necessary knowledge of its history.

The present state of the organisation

The next logical step in this journey of change is to be aware of present realities. This is especially important for those who do have a sense of the history of the system. The past should not be viewed through rose-tinted spectacles. There is nothing to be gained by harking back to a golden age, which may or may not have existed, and expecting that one-day it will return.

Reference has been made in preceding chapters to the prison colonies of the countries of the former Soviet Union. These were in effect, in Solzhenitsyn's term, a vast archipelago of labour camps, charged with making a major contribution to the economy of the USSR. The architecture of each camp, from Kaliningrad to Vladivostok, from the Arctic Circle to the Black Sea, was almost identical. Camps were divided into two sections, surrounded by a secure perimeter fence. One part was a series of large hostels, living units where prisoners spent the twelve hours each day when they were not working and where staff left them largely to their own devices. The second part was the power house of the colony, the reason for its existence, made up of a series of cavernous industrial workshops where prisoners laboured in two twelve hour shifts, six or seven days a week, fifty two weeks a year. With the break-up of the Soviet Union this great industrial complex has collapsed. There is no longer a guaranteed market for goods produced in the industrial workshops and this has meant that there is no steady income from their sale. This has had several consequences. One is that the whole balance of life in many of the colonies has been disrupted. The prisoners' daily routine of twelve hours hard labour and twelve hours left to their own devices has been broken. In some cases prisoners are still marched each day from the living part of the "zone" to the working part and left to fill their time as best they can in a desultory fashion. In other cases the majority are left in the cramped living accommodation with nothing to do, with the result that the dormitories have became breeding grounds for greater violence than before and for infectious diseases such as tuberculosis.

Another consequence of the post Soviet era is that in a number of countries resources have become very scarce. Under the Soviet regime the authorities in Moscow paid the salaries of the staff and all other expenses of the colonies were met from the profit made from the production lines. In a number of prison systems in Eastern Europe and Central Asia at present there is no guarantee that staff salaries will be paid regularly and there is very little income to meet other running expenses, let alone anything for capital investment. In another twist of the knife the central authorities still sometimes demand payment of the tax which was previously levied on profits from industrial production, even though the profits have actually disappeared.

These are the situations which still exist in many prison colonies in Eastern European and Central Asian countries. Yet many staff have not come to terms with this new reality. Anyone who has visited colonies, particularly those outside large cities, will be familiar with the situation described elsewhere by the present author (Coyle, 1999:60).

Previously many of the industrial work sheds in these camps operated round the clock. Now they stand empty. I found a typical example in a colony which I visited a few years ago in the north east of Kazakhstan. The series of work sheds were like great cathedrals, echoes of another era. They stood eerily silent with mountains of rusting machinery. In the distance shadowy figures floated in an out. In one corner a small number of prisoners were engaged on some minor repairs. The works manager who showed us round was still resplendent in full major's uniform, including highly polished knee length boots. He proudly told us how the machines had worked unceasingly in the past and how he always exceeded his production quota. He spoke with certainty, as if to convince himself, that these days would return if only the proper products could be identified.

The works manager paints a proud but sorry picture; a man coming to the close of his professional life, unable to admit something that he must know within himself to be true. He personifies the inability to recognise the new reality, which is that the great days of the past will not return. There has to be a new strategy for the organisation. It may well be that he himself is too steeped in the past to come to terms with this new agenda. If this is the case, he should be helped to come to accept his personal position and, if necessary, to retire with dignity. This subject was discussed in chapter two.

This personal trauma is often repeated at an organisational level. The system itself may be reluctant to accept that change of this sort is inevitable and may try to continue to operate within a context that is no longer relevant. In such a situation, there are several possible outcomes. While the organisation may continue to survive within an outdated context for a period, particularly if there are no immediate crises, change will inevitably come about. This may be as a result of external pressures from the government, from politicians or even through the media. Alternatively, it may be as a result of pressure from within the organisation, either from staff or from action taken by prisoners. One example of organisational change of this sort is to be found in the transfer of responsibility for prison administration from one government ministry to another, which was discussed in chapter three.

The prison systems of the countries of the former Soviet Union are extreme examples of the need to recognise that the models of imprisonment which exist in certain countries have become outdated and need to be re-constructed to take account of new realities. These countries are not alone in this predicament. In recent years in Central and Latin America, political changes in a number of countries have led to a recognition that models of imprisonment which existed under previous totalitarian governments and whose main purpose was to subdue the civilian population are no longer appropriate in a democratic society. In a number of these countries newly elected democratic leaders may well have personal experience of imprisonment under former regimes. Prison systems in Africa and in South Asia are also now beginning to throw off models of imprisonment which were imposed on them by colonial powers and are attempting to introduce models which are more suited to indigenous cultures (see for example Stern, 1999a). All of these prison systems are beginning to go through the dramatic challenge of converting their organisational models into ones that meet their present needs.

The pressures facing prison systems in some developed countries are less dramatic in style but no less fundamental. In many countries there has been a relentless diminution in recent years in the involvement of the state in managing central institutions. Governments no longer see themselves as having the prime responsibility for delivering education to young people or health care to sick people or social support to old people. In some cases this has all been delegated to the private sector to deliver either at market prices or on a subsidised basis. Most democratic states take the view that there are some elements of the society which should not be managed by the private sector but which should remain within the provenance of the states acting on behalf of its citizens. Typically, these will include the armed forces, the judiciary and the civil police. Until recently all states saw prison administration as a matter for central or local government control. They took the view that only the state had the right to deprive citizens of their liberty and with that went an obligation to look after them while in prison. Like defence of the nation, this was one state function which could not be delegated. This is no longer the case. In a number of countries, notably the United Kingdom, some states in Australia, some southern states in the United States and more recently New Zealand and South Africa, commercial companies have taken over the management of some prisons. A number of ethical questions have been raised about the propriety of the privatisation of prisons (Coyle et al., 2003). At this point we are only concerned with the implications for prison administrations.

Developments such as these have led some prison administrations to seek to apply criteria from the world of business and commerce to prison management. Prison governors and directors have been given annual targets to meet in terms of financial efficiency, of staff costs, of the number of escapes and serious incidents, and of the types of activities in which prisoners are involved. This has opened up a whole new set of questions about what kind of legitimate targets can be set for prison systems. One example, referred to in chapter three, is the extent to which prisons can be expected to have a role in helping a government reach its objective of reducing crime in civil society. The New Zealand Department of Corrections, for instance, has set itself the target of "reducing re-offending" (Department of Corrections, 2001:10).

All of these examples underline the fact that prisons and prison systems are affected by the wider social and political environment in which they exist. This environment may reinforce the existing culture of the organisation or it may challenge the traditional culture. The project steering group was told that the prison staff trade union in Sweden used employment legislation to challenge attempts by management to introduce new working practices. Similarly in England & Wales it has long been argued by some that the Prison Officers Association, which is the main staff trade union, has been able to exert a negative influence on the prison system by placing the narrow interests of its members before wider considerations such as the efficient running of the system, the rehabilitation of prisoners and even, on occasion, public safety. In the United States, the trade union representing correctional officers in California - the California Correctional Peace Officer's Association - has become one of the most powerful lobbying groups in the state.

The future direction of the organisation

Having acknowledged the history and also recognised the present reality, the next step is to decide the new direction that the organisation should take. Prison administrations will usually be part of a larger government department, such as the Ministry of the Interior or the Ministry of Justice. This department is likely to set goals or objectives for the prison system. It may also be responsible for providing financial and other resources. There will also be legislation within which the prison system has to operate. This is likely to include primary legislation such as a Penal Execution Code or a Prisons Act. In some jurisdictions this will be quite specific and prescriptive; this is the case in most countries in Eastern Europe and Central Asia. In other countries, such as the United Kingdom, the primary legislation will be couched in general terms and issues of detail will be dealt with by secondary legislation such as prison rules.

In addition to these national reference points there are a number of international ones which set standards for good prison management. The most important come from the United Nations. The main human rights instruments, such as the International Covenant on Civil and Political Rights, are legally binding international treaties which contain articles about the treatment of people who are deprived of their liberty. In addition, there are a number of international instruments that deal specifically with prisoners and conditions of detention. These include

- The Standard Minimum Rules for the Treatment of Prisoners (UN, 1957)

- The Body of Principles for the Protection of All Persons under Any Form of Detention or Imprisonment (UN, 1988)

- The Basic Principles for the Treatment of Prisoners (UN, 1990)

- The Standard Minimum Rules for the Administration of Juvenile Justice (UN, 1985)

There are also a number of instruments that refer specifically to staff working with people who have been deprived of their liberty. They include the Code of Conduct for Law Enforcement Officials (UN, 1979). For those in European jurisdictions there are also the European Prison Rules of the Council of Europe (1987). Although these international instruments do not have the force of law they have been accepted in principle by many state governments, which should therefore seek to implement them in their own jurisdictions.

These reference points are essential signposts for any prison system. Having decided that there has to be change, the international and national rules and regulations can be used as a framework for achieving this. The task which faces prison administrators is to put flesh on this framework. In doing so, other indicators will also have to be taken into account. For example, some governments are elected to power today with a strong agenda for law and order. One of the consequences of this political imperative may be an increase in the numbers of offenders being sent to prison, leaving the prison administration either to cope with increasing overcrowding or with having to find resources to build new prisons. In an age of decreased public spending, there is often an expectation that new initiatives should be implemented with no increase in resources, or even with less funding. All of these demands are likely to have significant influence on the future direction of any prison system as an organisation.

In deciding on important changes for any prison system and in setting a course to implement these changes a further important consideration which has already been referred to several times, has to be borne in mind. This is the crucial importance of the relationship between staff and prisoners. Between them, these two groups of people will have the greatest influence on whether the prison has a human or an inhuman environment and on whether the objectives set by national or local management can be realised. There are a number of other public sector organisations and institutions in which management is primarily about the treatment of human beings; schools and hospitals are obvious examples. They have many similarities with prisons in the way they need to be managed. What sets the prison apart is its coercive nature. Prisoners cannot choose to leave when they wish and their daily lives are circumscribed to a degree that does not happen in any other institution. This has a number of important implications for management.

A prison system which understands its history, which is capable of recognising its current situation and which acknowledges where it wants to get to has already begun the process of change. The next step is to develop a strategy for implementing change. This is the subject of the next chapter.

1   Personal communication with author.

5. Managing the change process

Prison management as a profession

Until quite recently most directors and governors of prisons did not recognise themselves as managers of what are often large and complex organisations. By the end of the twentieth century however, perceptions were changing. In 1991 the author of a report into the management of the Prison Service of England and Wales, who was himself an experienced businessman, wrote that:

> The Prison Service is the most complex organisation I have encountered and its problems some of the most intractable.
>
> **Lygo, 1991:2**

This development had been noted earlier in the United States of America. In his study of Stateville Penitentiary in Illinois, Jacobs observed that an incoming warden:

> … brought to the prison a commitment to scientific management rather than to any correctional ideology… He stresses efficient and emotionally detached management.
>
> **Jacobs, 1977:103-4**

In previous chapters we have shown that modern prison management requires a high degree of professional skill and awareness. It is important that this should be recognised and that the men and women who are placed in charge of prisons should be capable of management at a high level.

A number of prison systems have given a high priority in recent years to management issues. The Scottish Prison Service has identified four key elements in prison management: administrative, financial, human resources (covering both staff and prisoners) and operational. The conclusion reached by the Scottish Prison Service Board has been that the first three of these elements are common to all forms of management and that the operational element is the only one that is unique to the prison setting. As a consequence they have decided that prison governors and other members of the management team in a prison would benefit from a greater awareness of general management issues and how they are being tackled in other environments.

The National Agency for Correctional Institutions in the Netherlands has taken this a step further. Dutch prison directors are obliged to attend the generic management courses organised for all senior officials in the Ministry of Justice. The topics covered are strategic in orientation and cover issues such as the transformation of organisations, quality management and planning systems. This form of development has made prison directors more conscious of the fact that the prisons that they govern are part of a wider structure and that what happens in one part of the system can affect other parts. Key issues for consideration have been leadership, integrity and how to inspire and motivate staff. Less use has been made of management consultants and greater use of experts who are able to consider issues of principle and values. The main outcome of this approach has been a recognition that management in the public sector in general and in the prison system in particular is every bit as complex as management in the private sector.

The Swedish Prison and Probation Service has identified a particular need to develop the potential of middle managers. Throughout the 1990s the Swedish Service placed an emphasis on flattening the management structure, with four levels of staff under the head of the prison, made up of senior managers, unit managers, team leaders and staff members. The unit managers have a key role in this structure. The original intention had been to recruit highly qualified persons from outside the service to take on these roles but this initiative has not been successful and so the alternative has been to train these managers inside the service.

In public sector organisations in many countries the last decade has been marked by an emphasis on managerial issues. The world of prisons has not been exempt from this development. To use its own terminology, this "managerialism" usually involves a focus on what are called processes and outputs rather than on outcomes. In common language, this means a concentration on how things are done and what the organisation achieves rather than on the changes which result from the activities of the organisation. There is much to be said for such an approach. Properly used, it can ensure that organisations run more efficiently, that they are cost effective and that they produce what is expected of them. Nevertheless, it is important to recognise its limitations, especially in a prison system.

If one accepts the contention that prisons are places where the relationships between the human beings involved have a central role to play in determining both culture and organisational direction, an important conclusion follows. This is the need for prisons to operate within an ethical context. If one loses sight of this, there is a real danger that the perfectly proper insistence on performance targets and process delivery will encourage the ever-present danger of forgetting that the prison service is not the same as a factory which produces motor cars or washing machines. The management of prisons is primarily about the management of human beings, both staff and prisoners. This means that there are issues that go beyond effectiveness and efficiency. When making decisions about the treatment of human beings there is a more radical consideration. The first question which must always be asked when considering any new managerial initiative is, "Is it right?".

From a purely managerial perspective the prison system which existed in the former Soviet Union was a model of efficiency. If the prisons and colonies in the GULAG had been measured by modern performance indicators, they would have passed with flying colours. There were virtually no escapes because the penalty of a failed attempt was death. There were few assaults on staff because perpetrators would have faced severe reprisals. As far as the organisation was concerned, the priority for the colony was to deliver a high level of industrial production. This was a simple message for the director of the colony and he made sure that it was delivered. The question "Is it right?" was nowhere on the agenda. The same could be said of countless other places of detention in totalitarian states.

These considerations also apply to prisons and places of detention in democratic countries. One conclusion to be drawn from reading the reports produced, for example, by the CPT is that those responsible for the management of prisons and those who work in them need to avoid taking a purely technocratic approach to their work. It is not sufficient to measure success or failure merely in managerial terms, divorced from any consideration of what effect this has on the people involved, both staff and prisoners. One of the first consequences of such an approach will be that one loses sight of the fact that all the players, including and especially prisoners, are human beings.

In managerial terms it is important that processes and outputs in prisons should be managed efficiently and effectively so as to meet the legitimate expectations of governments, of civil society, of victims and of staff, prisoners and their families. If it is true that prisons reflect the most central values of a society, it is even more important that those with responsibility for prisons and prison systems should look beyond technical and managerial considerations. They also have to be leaders who are capable of enthusing the staff for whom they are responsible with a sense of decency in the way they carry out their difficult daily tasks. If this happens, it is more likely that the "outcomes" from the prison will be of benefit to all members of society.

Leadership

In the course of this book we have been drawn inexorably towards a recognition of the crucial nature of leadership in the prison world. The importance of leadership runs throughout every level of the system. It begins in individual prisons where the character of the person in charge can be decisive in setting the culture of the establishment. Reference has already been made to the importance of personal relationships in the prison setting and the extent to which the success or failure of managerial initiatives depends on the nature of these relationships between prisoners, staff and all other people involved in the prison. Prison systems are hierarchical organisations and all of those involved in them will tend to look to the person at the top for a lead as to what is expected in terms of attitude, behaviour and manner of working. The prisons with the most humane atmosphere, with the most positive culture, are likely to be those with the most visible leadership. It is also important to recognise that strong leadership is also more likely to produce efficient security systems and a safe environment.

This leadership can be demonstrated in a number of ways. A strong leader will generally have a recognisable charisma, which will attract trust and confidence from staff. If the leadership is genuine, it will also be linked to organisational ability in a way that ensures that it does not degenerate into idiosyncrasy. The best leaders are likely to use a style of management that can be described as "tight and loose". That is, they will place great emphasis on the ethos within which the prison should operate and will set very clear parameters about what is to be done and what kind of behaviour is acceptable and what is not. Having done that, the leaders will then encourage staff at lower levels to use their initiative in implementing the details of the agreed policy.

This issue of trust is an important one in the prison setting. We suggested in chapter three that in some settings the success of a prison may be measured by absence of failure. Success, at least in the eyes of the public and often of politicians, is when there are no escape, no riots, no serious disturbances, no suicides. If success is to be measured in such a negative manner, it is understandable that prison directors and other senior managers will place a greater emphasis on ensuring that mistakes are not made, rather than on giving a priority to innovative ways of working which may bring about change but which also carry a degree of risk. What this means in practice is that senior management frequently does not trust its staff and spends most of its energies on preventing failures rather than on encouraging success. A real leader will have the confidence to hit the proper balance between the two and will imbue staff with a sense of belief in their own ability.

This confidence has to stretch up through the wider organisation as well as down to junior staff of each prison. One of the functions of the prison director as leader is to protect the organisation of his or her prison from inappropriate external interference from national or regional headquarters, even when this is meant to be benign. We have already discussed how individual prisons have to operate as part of a national or regional system and to observe legislation, rules and regulations, but they also need to have their own individual dynamism. A national prison system has to follow the broad policy set by government and has to ensure that this is implemented at local level. But central administrators should not attempt to be super-prison directors, determining the detail of what happens in each individual prison. An attempt to impose such a way of working is likely to lead to an inefficient organisation.

All of these considerations imply that the governor as leader must also be highly visible within his or her prison. Hardly a day should go past without the head of the prison being seen in all areas where prisoners and staff come together. This visibility should be seen as supportive rather than inspectorial, particularly by staff. It will encourage committed staff to devote themselves wholeheartedly to their work. It will, of course, also have the effect of ensuring that staff who might otherwise hide in offices or behind the ever-present paperwork do not do so. Directors and governors who regularly meet staff and prisoners in the various corners of the prison will have a much better feel for the culture of their organisation. This also means that heads of prisons and other senior members of management should not restrict their attendance to week-day office hours. In many systems the days when directors and other staff were required to live in accommodation provided on the prison compound have largely passed but there are still strong arguments for expecting directors to live in relative proximity to their prisons so that they can be on site quickly in case of an emergency and are able to visit the prison early in the morning, late in the evening, at night and at weekends.

The hierarchy of the prison extends beyond individual establishments to the service as a whole and in the same way the principles of leadership need to extend to the whole prison system. In many jurisdictions the most senior officials in the prison system are not career prison persons. They may, for example, come from the wider civil service. In these circumstances appointment to head the prison system is seen as simply another step on the senior civil service ladder. In other jurisdictions it is not uncommon to find a recently retired senior military officer leading the prison system. More frequently now than previously, one finds that prison systems are led by men or women with a professional prison background. What is clear from an examination of the way that various prison systems are led is that the immediate professional background of the person in charge is less important than his or her leadership qualities. Successful prison managers are those who are able to inspire the staff for whom they are responsible while retaining the confidence of the government ministers and senior administrators who have appointed them.

Vision

If successful radical change is to be achieved within a prison system, something more than efficient administration is required. The world of the prison is a multi-layered complexity. It is coercive in that one of the tasks of staff is to make sure that prisoners do not leave the prison without proper authority. It is disciplined in that there should be good order at all times. It is developmental in that staff should help prisoners to learn skills and develop habits that will lead to a change in their way of life. All of these tasks need to be carried out within an environment which is decent and humane, in which individuals, whether their uniform be that of staff or prisoner, are respected in their own right as human beings and in which there is total respect for the law. It is relatively easy to produce a series of targets to cover a whole range of factors from the number of escapes to the number of prisoners who have undertaken an education course. It is much more difficult to produce targets that measure humanity and decency and to enthuse staff with a commitment to carry out their work in a professional and dedicated manner.

This is more likely to happen in a prison system which has a clear vision of what it hopes to achieve and which communicates that clearly to everyone involved, staff and prisoners. In large organisations it is often useful to find a method of articulating the vision in a brief statement which attempts to encapsulate the key features which set the organisation apart from all others. In modern organisational language these are often called 'Mission Statements'. As an example, the one used by the Scottish Prison service is:

> The Mission of the Scottish Prison Service is:
>
> - to keep in custody those committed by the Courts;
>
> - to maintain good order in each prison;
>
> - to care for prisoners with humanity; and
>
> - to provide prisoners with a range of opportunities to exercise personal responsibility and to prepare for release.

This statement is frequently referred to by staff as "COCO", a reference to the key words: custody, order, care and opportunity. This is a useful way of giving a clear message about the main aims of the organisation. In England and Wales staff used to be issued with a similar statement on a small piece of adhesive paper which had to be affixed to the back of the personal identity card carried at all times by every member of staff. A number of other prison systems use similar stratagems to maintain staff awareness of the special nature of their task.

Of themselves, mission statements have little meaning unless they are a genuine expression of the context within which all activities are to be undertaken. Providing a vision for an organisation is a method of helping its members to step back from the daily grind and to place their work within a wider context. If a prison system has a vision about what it is trying to achieve, it is more likely to be able to remember that the managerial processes to which we referred previously, no matter how important they may be in relative terms, are merely means to an end and not an end in themselves. In any organisation such a vision will come in the first instance from the most senior people, who should be in a position to place the organisation itself within a wider setting. Within the prison setting, this vision may come from those with political responsibility, such as government ministers, but it may more often be the responsibility of those at the most senior official level, Directors General, Commissioners and their senior management colleagues. At local level this role will fall on prison directors and governors.

Staff/Prisoner relationships

There is a need to keep reinforcing the fact that prisons are dynamic institutions in which the most important elements are human beings. They are not inanimate entities made up solely of buildings, walls and fences. Their success or failure cannot be managed merely by means of a series of set formulae, calculated by a national administration or government department. The human element has to be taken into account at every step. Real change in any prison system cannot take root without the involvement of both staff and prisoners. That fact has always been recognised by those who understand the dynamics of any prison. Governments come and go and their policies may change. Directors of prison systems come and go and their visions may change. Key performance indicators and targets may be set and re-set. Yet there are only three constant features in any prison system: the **prison** itself in which **prisoners** are held and the **prison staff** who look after them. The key feature for the success or failure of any prison system that is to be run in a decent and humane manner is the relationship between prisoners and the prison staff with whom they come into contact on a daily basis. This means, first of all, the uniformed staff who unlock prisoners in the morning and lock them up last thing at night. In between times they deal with prisoners when they are at their best and at their worst, at their strongest and at their weakest. There is a relationship of mutual dependency between prisoners and prison staff. One group cannot exist without the other. Between them they can have the greatest influence on whether the prison has a human or an inhuman environment and on whether the objectives set by national or local management can be realised.

On a day to day basis what makes prison life either tolerable or unbearable for prisoners is their relationship with staff. Any attempt to change the culture of a prison or of a prison system has to recognise this fact. This also underlines the reality that prisoners are not mere passive players in this scenario. They must be actively involved in the organisation. This is not to deny the fact that staff have to control the routine of the prison. However, it has to be acknowledged that all the internal players in the prison, prisoners as well as staff need to be treated with respect.

An interesting feature of this dynamic, which is frequently overlooked, is the extent to which staff and prisoners can have what almost amounts to a rivalry in competing for the attention of senior management and the head of the prison in particular. If too much attention is paid to the needs of the prisoners it sometimes happens that staff become aggrieved, feeling that their needs are being overlooked. Similarly, prisoners may react in a negative fashion if they feel that the director or governor is continually siding with the staff. In these circumstances the head of the prison has an important role to play in brokering a balanced relationship between staff and prisoners.

Having said that, it should never be forgotten that prisons are primarily hierarchical institutions in which everyone has his or her place. It is important to know what the boundaries are and not to overstep them. The punishment for doing so is usually swift and, importantly, may well come not from the "other side" but from one's own side. Prisoners' retribution against the "grass", the prisoner who sides with staff, is well known. What may be less appreciated is that there is an equally unforgiving code of conduct among staff, which deals swiftly with any colleague who supports the "other side" by stepping out of line, for example, to draw attention to the fact that a prisoner has been unfairly or illegally treated. In the closed world of the prison this structure is monolithic and difficult to break down. If there is to be real culture change in a prison this structure has to be changed in a manner which breaks down the barriers between staff and prisoners without threatening the legitimate needs of security and good order. This radical change will only come about if those responsible for prison systems are determined in their efforts and leave junior staff in no doubt about what is expected of them. In achieving this, the first thing is to make use of the hierarchical nature of the organisation. Prison systems are primarily disciplined institutions. Most staff make much of this; in many countries they enjoy having military ranks; they draw parallels between themselves and the police. One of the key features of an organisation which gives a high priority to its disciplined nature is that staff are accustomed to obeying orders. This also applies in the prison system and can be used to advantage in bringing about change.

In developing a strategy to change the culture in an organisation like a prison system, one often has to adopt a pragmatic approach. Ultimately, real change will come about when attitudes alter, but this is not likely to happen immediately. In the first instance it may be necessary to insist on a change in behaviour, in what staff do. In its most direct form this may involve saying to some staff, "We can do nothing at this stage about what you think, but we insist that this is the new way in which you will have to behave." Initially this is likely to involve a prohibition on negative behaviour: no violence, no bullying, no racial or sexual harassment. It will then move to an insistence on positive behaviour such as the manner in which prisoners are spoken to and the way they are treated. It may well happen that some staff will at first respond to such an approach by ignoring instructions, even when they are quite direct. In the past they may well have discovered that this is a good way of testing the extent to which the person who has issued the order really expects it to be obeyed. If no one comes back to check, then it may be that the order was given for purely cosmetic reasons and real change was not intended. If the order is reinforced, the next step will probably be for the doubting member of staff to check if the order really was issued and was intended to be followed. For these doubting members of staff the final step may be for the director or governor to make it clear to the individuals concerned that they must observe the order which has been given. When it comes to this, even the most reluctant member of staff knows that in a disciplined service a direct order that is reinforced cannot be ignored. The vast majority of staff will be quite prepared to take their lead from the top and to follow clear instructions. But they need to be confident that management will follow through on the desire for change and will not retreat when faced with difficulties. They also need to see that the small number of staff who do not wish to change will not be left to carry on in their own way.

Staff attitudes

In the longer term simply changing behaviour is not enough. If the culture of a prison or a prison system is to be fundamentally altered there also has to be a change of attitude on the part of staff. Most prison staff wish to do their work well and in a professional manner. Many of them will have joined the prison system because they wish to work in a public service. Others will have joined because of the prospect of long term secure employment. A few may have joined because they expected to have the opportunity to wield power over other human beings. In the course of their careers they may have come to the conclusion that success in the prison service is measured in negative terms. The important thing is to make sure that no prisoner escapes and that there are no major violent incidents. In the course of daily activities, the important thing is to have a quiet life: "A good day is a day when nothing happens". For these staff a good prisoner is a quiet prisoner. It would have been one of them who coined the phrase, "Happiness is door-shaped", meaning that the most satisfying part of a prison officer's day is when all the prisoners are safely locked up. If the negative culture of the prison is to be converted into something more positive, the attitude of staff to their work and to prisoners needs to be positive.

One often finds that the staff who are most resistant to change are not necessarily those with the longest service. In the course of the fieldwork undertaken for writing this book it was suggested several times that the most problematic group of staff includes some that are relatively young and have been in the job for a few years. The first survey of prison staff in England & Wales, carried out in 1982, found the most negative reaction coming from staff aged 31-35 years with about five years service, while the most positive reaction was from older staff who had other work/life experiences (OPCS, 1985). The Scottish Prison Service survey of 1998 identified a disaffected group of staff with six to eight years service (Wozniak, 1998). The description "dinosaur", which is frequently used to describe staff who have an inflexible attitude, does not necessarily apply exclusively to older or more experienced staff.

The Director General of the Swedish Prison and Probation Service, at the time of the fieldwork for this book, was a former General in the Swedish Army. He recognised the pseudo-military nature of the prison service and took advantage of this in insisting on the need for change from the top. At the same time, he pointed out that in the prison service, just as in the military, routine can lead to sloppiness of direction, with senior management concentrating on management rather than leadership. One consequence of the absence of firm direction is that a small number of obstructive staff can have an undue influence, both on their colleagues and on the culture of prison. These people may well set themselves up as custodians of tradition. Government policies will change, prison directors will come and go they argue, but we will always be here and we are the real experts on what can and cannot be achieved in the prison setting. It is this attitude which gave rise to the aphorism which was heard several times in Sweden: "The culture of this prison is in the walls".

In some respects, prisons are monolithic insensitive organisations where concerns of the individual are subservient to those of the whole. At another level they are extremely sensitive to small indicators. They are places of great symbolism where words and descriptions mean much more than their face value. For example, terminology in the prison world is an important indicator of the presence or absence of humanity. The application of terminology to prisoners is referred to in the following chapter on what constitutes a good prison. It is also relevant in respect of staff.

The Prison Service of England & Wales provides a good case study in respect of the issue of staff identification. In the early 1990s national management decided that all staff should wear name badges so that they could be identified by prisoners and by visitors to the prison. This initiative was taken in the interests of staff as much as anyone else. A frequent complaint made by staff was that they were never seen as individuals but rather as "the officer", "the PO" (Principal Officer) or "the Governor". The instruction to staff to wear name badges began as a recommendation, something to be encouraged, and many staff responded positively. In 1993 an order was issued that all staff should immediately wear their name badges. The Prison Officers' Association, the main staff trade union, saw this as an opportunity to oppose the new senior management and issued an instruction to all their members not to wear badges, using the argument that if prisoners got to know the names of staff they might find out where they lived and get associates to threaten them or their families. This became a focus for other staff dissatisfaction and many staff who had previously been wearing their badges stopped doing so. National management decided not to pursue the issue and no action was taken. In 2000 the issue again came to the fore, this time because of concern at staff abuse in some prisons, when it was not possible to identify staff who had taken part in incidents in which prisoners were physically abused. Management's compromise was that all staff would wear badges, not with their names, but with numbers. The trade union did not object to this arrangement and it has now been introduced. This compromise is actually a retrogressive step since it seems to suggest that both staff and prisoners are to be regarded as ciphers rather than as individual human beings.

The reluctance on the part of prison staff in England to wear name badges was not because of a real fear of being identified by prisoners. Prisoners invariably know the names of most of the staff with whom they come into daily contact, just as staff know the names of prisoners. Instead, it was a reflection of the general attitude of many staff to prison service management. Just as some staff have a "them and us" attitude to prisoners, so they have a similar attitude to prison management. This symbiotic attitude to management is reinforced by the tradition in a number of prison systems that junior staff wear uniforms while senior staff wear civilian clothes. Management are frequently referred to by the pejorative description, "the suits". Uniformed staff who deal directly with prisoners often feel that only they have a real understanding of the mentality of prisoners and that their working life is made much more complicated by the unrealistic and naive attitude adopted by senior staff towards prisoners. This attitude may persist even when senior staff have themselves risen through the ranks of uniformed staff.

The explanations of this defensive attitude can be found in wider perceptions of the role of the prison officer. Prison staff often regard themselves as the forgotten members of the criminal justice system. Traditionally they have sought comparison with police officers. One way of seeking this has been to claim parity of pay, as has frequently happened in the United Kingdom without success. In Eastern European structures this has been at the root of the desire of prison staff to remain within the Ministry of the Interior, alongside the police. Yet in the eyes of the public and of governments, prison staff lag well behind the police in terms of status and public recognition. Prison staff in many countries feel aggrieved that the police have such a high public standing even though their task is merely to identify and to arrest serious criminals. Prison staff would argue that their role, that of keeping these convicted criminals under lock and key for many years, is a much more demanding and dangerous one. Sometimes prison staff even sense that the public identify all of those behind the walls of the prison, whether prisoners or staff, as having pariah status. They are frustrated and angry that this should be the case. There are two ways of expressing this frustration. The first is by treating the prisoners in a way which emphasises that they, the staff, have a moral superiority over them. The second is by making the lives of management difficult, usually through indirect obstruction of their initiatives. The only suitable response to this defensive mentality is by giving prison staff a greater sense of professional worth and appreciation of the value of the role which they carry out on behalf of society.

Recruitment and training of staff

In 1999 the International Centre for Prison Studies carried out a review on behalf of the Prison Service of England & Wales of the induction training given to newly recruited prison officers. One of the most important conclusions of this review was that there was a lack of clarity about what staff were being trained to do. The English Prison Service is by no means the only prison system which faces the uncertainty which arises, at least in part, from the complex nature of the role of the prison officer. A role which involves enforcing security, maintaining good order and helping prisoners to reform themselves. It takes a very special person to carry out all of these functions in a competent and professional fashion. Great care needs to be taken in recruiting the right people, in giving them proper initial training and in ensuring that they continue to develop their skills throughout their career.

Although the proper role of the modern prison officer is very complex, this is often not recognised in the methods used to recruit staff. In some countries priority is given to the security aspect of the work and newly recruited staff are merely regarded as guards. In this case, when training is given it is likely to be restricted to the proper use of weapons of control, be they rifles or pistols or only batons and sticks. In countries where young men have to spend a year or so undergoing national service, it may be that this time can be spent as a prison guard. In this case the conscripts are often little more than teenagers, younger than many of the prisoners of whom they have charge. An additional consequence of this arrangement is that there will be a very high turnover of staff. In other countries a large proportion of staff may be former members of the armed services, enhancing their army pension by working as prison guards. It may be that people who have been unsuccessful in an application to work in the police service turn to the prison service as a second-best option and then view their work primarily as control.

The likelihood of recruiting high quality staff is often affected by the location of a prison. Prisons are frequently constructed away from the urban areas from which most prisoners come. It is unlikely that prisons will be established in high amenity areas or within communities where there is high employment. In England, Dartmoor prison was built in the early nineteenth century on the edge of a Devon moor, far from centres of population, to house French prisoners of war. It is still in use today. The maximum-security prison for the state of New York is in the small town of Attica close to the Canadian border. The vast majority of the prisoners held there come from New York City, hundreds of miles to the south. The Scottish equivalent of this is Peterhead prison, built in the part of Scotland which stretches furthest into the North Sea, holding prisoners who come mainly from the populated areas of the country several hundred miles to the south. Many of the prison colonies in Eastern Europe and Central Asia were deliberately built far from centres of population in order to emphasise the separation of the prisoner from his or her community. In other instances, the location of a prison may be determined not by the concept of exile but because of the need to provide local employment.

A series of circumstances such as this, in which people work in prison either by default, or because they were previously in the military, or because they have failed in their desire to work as police, or simply because there is no other work available, and in which there may a cultural divide between prisoners and prison staff has another important consequence. It is that prison staff, either through genuine fear of an unknown group of people or in order to impress their families and acquaintances about the environment in which they work, will demonise the prisoners for whom they are responsible. They will foster a myth that these are extremely dangerous people, that those who work with them are protecting the public from unspeakable danger and that they, the prison staff, face continuous physical threat. This attitude is understandable if one considers examples, such as Kumla Prison in Sweden, where the staff recruited to work in the new prison were already feeling devalued at being made redundant from their skilled jobs as shoe-makers or train engineers and had to find a way of justifying to themselves that what they were now being asked to do was of equal importance. The same consideration applies where the prison personnel had originally wanted to have jobs, such as policemen or women, which would give them respect in their communities.

The reality is that when the time comes for students to leave high schools or universities the notion of working in a prison is rarely considered. By and large, men and women gravitate towards prison work either by default or because it is a means of entering public service without qualifications. If there is to be a serious attempt to establish prison work as a proper career of which one can be proud and for which one has to be professionally trained, there has to be a proper appreciation of the sort of person who should be recruited to carry out this work.

Once the appropriate staff have been recruited and selected, they then have to be properly trained. If one accepts that work in the prison system is indeed a form of public service, this will affect the nature of the training that is to be given to staff. In the first instance, one can relate this to training given to public servants in similar fields of work. This has been one of the key messages being implemented in training arrangements for prison staff in the Netherlands. Rather than create separate dedicated training institutes, the National Agency for Correctional Institutions has made use of standard vocational training available in general training facilities and educational institutes, where prison officers get approximately the same type of training as people working in mental health care, child care or other social services. This has the added benefit of making the work of the prison officers a more respected job and more comparable with other professions. This is not, of course, to say that the work of the prison officer is exactly the same as that of the mental health nurse, the teacher or the social worker. There are specific elements, such as the requirement to be conscious of security considerations, which make the role of the prison officer unique; but these unique features have to be considered within the context of those elements which are common to people working in similar professions. These common features are arguably more important than the security considerations which invite comparisons with police or even military personnel.

If the way in which new staff are trained is an important element in changing the culture of a prison system, there are also other important factors which must not be overlooked. These include the environment in which training is to be delivered and the personnel who are to be entrusted with this important duty. In a number of countries prison staff are trained in annexes of Ministry of the Interior training centres or of police academies. The training in this environment is likely to take on militaristic overtones, with the highlight being the final passing out parade before a senior military figure. This message will be reinforced if the trainers are themselves former soldiers or policemen, whose main aim is to instil a sense of discipline into new recruits. Prison staff do need to have a disciplined approach to their work. Theirs is a hierarchical world in which people have to know how to take orders and how to give them at the appropriate time. But good prison management depends on much more than an ability to give or to receive orders. It is primarily about an ability to manage people. Even the most junior members of the prison staff will quickly find themselves in a situation where they are required to manage prisoners in a manner which goes far beyond the simple issuing of an order. New recruits are more likely to learn the skills necessary for their complex tasks in an environment which is disciplined yet which encourages questioning and the use of initiative. The prison officer will probably never be required to take part in another ceremonial parade after leaving the initial training centre. Instead, he or she will regularly have to call on newly acquired skills in order to help the people for whom they are responsible to make good use of their time in prison. This means the ability to see people as individuals, rather than as numbers; as human beings, rather than solely as prisoners.

This is are very complex set of skills to teach new recruits, many of whom will have had no prior experience of managing difficult human beings. The senior members of staff whose task it is to instil these skills into new recruits should be carefully chosen. In some countries the reality is that work in the prison staff training centre is seen as a refuge for senior members of staff who have grown weary of working in prisons, or been burned out, or who simply have been found not capable of doing the job. They are entrusted with passing on to new recruits a set of skills that they themselves do not have. The lessons that they teach bear little relation to the reality that the recruits will soon experience. In an environment such as this, it is not strange that having successfully completed initial training and been posted to a prison, the first thing new officers are told is to forget everything that they have learned so far and to regard their training as starting at that point. In the Prison Service of England & Wales this problem is overcome by selecting some of the best young senior officers, that is, those who have achieved their first promotion, to teach in the training college for a few years. They will then expect to return to work in a prison with a further promotion. In other words, being a trainer for a number of years is a recognised career route for the best staff rather than an escape for those older staff who have had enough of working in prisons.

There are many generic features to the work of the prison officer, which remain the same wherever he or she is working, and these can be communicated to all new recruits. However, there are also a wide variety of skills that are specific to particular settings. Additional skills are needed when working with young prisoners, with women prisoners, in low security and in high security prisons. Much of the initial training given to staff is aimed at those who will work with adult male prisoners with, at best, a short session or two given to the special skills needed for working with other groups. Working in maximum-security prisons often carries a special cachet and is regarded by many staff as the most demanding. In some instances this may indeed be the case but very often a much higher level of skill is required to work, for example, with volatile young offenders. However, frequently this work does not attract the same attention, nor appropriate levels of training.

In all professional work there is a constant need for updating training and for encouraging development of principles and practice. This also applies in respect to work in prisons. If this is to be more than merely a reactive task, driven by security and waiting to deal with things once they have gone wrong, prison staff need to be given regular opportunities to upgrade their knowledge and skills and to learn about new developments. This is likely to require close links between senior prison training staff and those in other public sectors; these will include experts in criminal justice, academics, public service administrators, management theorists and human rights lawyers.

All of this assumes that those involved in prison work and those who are responsible for prison systems do in fact regard such work as professional, on a par with that of other public sector professional staff. If this is to be more than lip-service, the implication is that new prison staff need to be properly selected, assessed and trained and that throughout their career they need to be given the opportunity to expand and develop their skills. If this does not happen then they are likely to remain one of the most undervalued sectors of public employees.

Now that we have considered some of the most important elements in the process of managing change within prisons, we can turn our attention to the outcome of this process. What are the main features that characterise good prison management?

6. The outcome: what constitutes good prison management?

The principles

We have now reached the stage at which we can consider the essential elements of good prison management. We can begin by stating the obvious and reminding ourselves that when people are sent to prison they retain all of their basic rights as human beings. In the words of a famous English judgement, "in spite of his imprisonment, a convicted prisoner retains all civil rights which are not taken away expressly or by necessary implication" (Wilberforce 1983:10).

These rights can be summarised under the following headings:

- Maintenance of human dignity: the rights to freedom from torture and inhuman, cruel or degrading treatment, to proper accommodation, hygiene facilities, clothing and bedding, to sufficient food and water, to sufficient exercise and fresh air.

- Proper health care.

- Personal safety: that the level of security should be sufficient to ensure the safety of the public but should not be oppressive; that no-one in prison should be at risk of physical, sexual or mental abuse; that internal procedures for discipline and punishment should observe the tenets of natural justice.

- Contact with families, friends and the outside world should be of a quantity and quality that allows the maintenance and development of proper relationships.

- Access to a range of activities: work, education, cultural activities, physical exercise, observance of religion.

- Access to necessary legal representation for those who are awaiting trial, sentence or appeal and also for those who have legitimate complaints about their treatment.

- Respecting the needs of special categories of prisoners, such as women, juveniles and other minority groups.

A well managed prison is one in which all of the above rights are delivered.

In chapter four reference was made to the whole range of international human rights instruments which confirm that general human rights standards should also be applied to those who are in prison. A useful reference document for the United Nations instruments is the Manual on Human Rights Training for Prison Officials, published by the Office of the UN High Commissioner for Human Rights in Geneva (UNHCHR 2000). The European Prison Rules (Council of Europe 1987) are another very useful point of reference.

In most democratic countries there is acceptance in general terms that all of these principles should be respected in the prison environment. When it comes to the application of specific principles there may well be problems. In the European context, for example, both the Commission and the Court of Human Rights (now unified as the Court of Human Rights) have passed down decisions covering such issues as the right of prisoners to private correspondence and to marry.

The International Centre for Prison Studies has recently published a handbook on prison management which describes how the international human rights instruments can be used as a tool for the development of a model of prison management (Coyle 2002). This handbook describes the essentials of good prison management. Among all of the factors mentioned above, there are a number of significant elements which are useful pointers to whether or not a prison is well managed. These include the following.

The physical environment

Prisons are physical institutions, made up of buildings in particular locations. One of the first tasks of the good prison manager is to make the best possible use of available accommodation. Reference was made in chapter two to the problems of overcrowding which exist in many countries, particularly the way in which this affects prisoners' living space. The control of overcrowding within a prison system as a whole cannot be dealt with by individual prison directors. It is the responsibility of the national prison administration and ultimately of the government. At a technical level the problem of prison overcrowding can be resolved if the national administration ensures that enough spaces are provided by building new prisons.

There are two important caveats to this. The first is that little evidence from any country that prison administrations can build themselves out of overcrowding. In the early years of the twentieth century an English Prison Commissioner wrote, "Wherever prisons are built, Courts will make use of them" (Ruck 1951:26). All the indications are that in the years since this statement was written, things have not changed. New prison accommodation almost invariably is followed by further rises in the number of people being sent to prison. The second caveat is that new prison building is an expensive option, which is unlikely to be available in any but the most affluent countries.

In the longer term the best solution to prison overcrowding is that judges should be asked to look closely at the need to send people to prison and that legislators should show a lead in restricting the availability of prison as a punishment for any but the most serious crimes. Those responsible for prison administration should not encourage an expansionist approach to imprisonment.

In the shorter term, prison administrators should make sure that the available accommodation is put to most efficient use. It is noticeable that in most prison systems overcrowding is spread unevenly. Technically the Russian prison system is only 2% overcrowded (World Prison Brief 2002). This bald statistic hides the fact that some prisons are overcrowded by up to 300%. Those with the worst overcrowding tend to be the largest prisons. This must mean that many other prisons have unused accommodation. The reason for this is that overcrowding is generally concentrated among certain groups of prisoners, usually those awaiting trial and sometimes particular groups of convicted prisoners, such as those serving shorter sentences. Various operational reasons can be offered for this uneven distribution of prisoners. One may be the need to keep certain groups of prisoners, such as those awaiting trial, separate from others and available for interview by investigative or judicial authorities. Another may be the need for some prisoners to be kept in prisons with a high level of security. Despite legal and other restrictions, it should be possible for prison administrations to arrange the overall use of accommodation in such a way that, where overcrowding has to exist, its effects are minimised by being spread as evenly as possible.

At the level of individual prisons, directors need to be ready to make optimum use of every area in the prison. The greatest effect of overcrowding is usually felt in the actual living accommodation. However, in many prisons, even in some of those with high levels of over-population, there are significant areas of the prison which are not fully utilised. The majority of prisoners may well be required to spend 22 or 23 hours each day in the overcrowded living areas while work units, classrooms, chapels or other places of prayer, exercise yards and even large corridors lie unused for most of the time. During the early 1990s the present author was in charge of one of the main London prisons. It was significantly over-crowded and prisoners spent much of each day in their cells because of shortage of other areas for them to go to work, for education or for other activities. Yet in this cramped prison there were two large Christian chapels which were only used for a couple of hours each week. The first task was to convince the Anglican and the Catholic authorities that they should share a single chapel, so that the other one could be put to other use. The next task was to convince both authorities that when the remaining chapel was not being used for worship it should be available for a variety of other activities, just as happens with many churches in the community.

There are many other examples of finding ways to make use of available space. In one prison in West Africa the new director found that prisoners were only allowed to go into the large yard in small numbers because the wall of the prison was low enough to tempt them to escape. The majority of prisoners had to spend all day locked in overcrowded rooms. For relatively little expenditure the new director was able to secure funds to build the brick wall to a height which meant that he could allow all prisoners out of their cells for most of the day. In some overcrowded prisons in Russia areas on the flat roofs of buildings have been converted so that prisoners can take part in a variety of activities there.

Even where overcrowding does not exist or where it is kept to a minimum, the overall size of a prison is important. It is difficult to help individuals to make major changes in their lives if they live in large institutions. Given the number of people who are in prison today in most countries, it is not practical to hold them in small prisons, although one does find this from time to time. Nevertheless, one can reach some conclusions about optimum numbers for prisons to hold. The biggest prisons in the world hold up to 10,000 prisoners. Kresty in St Petersburg and Tihar in New Delhi have already been referred to. Others, such as Rikers Island in New York City, hold even larger numbers in a complex which is in fact several jails. In some of the countries with the highest rates of imprisonment it is common to find prisons with anything between 2,000 and 9,000 prisoners. One can say with a reasonable degree of confidence that from an operational perspective it is impossible to manage a single entity prison of this size in a decent and humane fashion. The roll-call of riots and inhumanity in many of these monolithic prisons bears testimony to that.

In managerial terms it is possible to manage prisons of up to 500 prisoners in a manner which takes some account of the individual needs of prisoners, although experience suggests that ideally the number should be no more than 200 or 300. The length of stay for prisoners is also an important factor in this equation. If there are dozens of prisoners being released or transferred or being admitted each day it will be difficult for staff to get to know them as individuals. On the other hand, it may be possible to achieve this with a population of up to 500 if there is relatively little turnover in prisoners and staff. There are also management techniques which can make this more feasible, such as breaking the total population into sub-groups of 50 or so, with identified staff looking after them in a semi-autonomous manner. There is little doubt that if the numbers in a prison go beyond a thousand there is virtually no possibility of dealing with the needs of individual prisoners in other than a superficial manner.

Decency and humanity

Inhumanity in a prison is often the result of a combination of factors. For example, when the Council of Europe Committee for the Prevention of Torture and Inhuman or Degrading Treatment or Punishment (CPT) visited England in 1990 it concluded that in the three main prisons which it visited, Brixton, Leeds and Wandsworth, a combination of negative features amounted to inhuman and degrading treatment of the prisoners who were held in these prisons (CPT 1991a). In the first place, there was overcrowding, with two or three prisoners regularly held in small cells intended to hold one prisoner. The resulting high number of prisoners meant that the infrastructure of the prison could not cope and in particular the level of sanitation, with limited access to toilet and washing facilities, was unacceptable. Finally, there was very little daily activity for the prisoners, who had to spend the vast majority of the day in the small cells. The English prison administration recognised that there was overcrowding, that there was poor sanitation and that there was little activity for prisoners. Nevertheless, it was reluctant to accept the view of the CPT that this amounted to inhuman and degrading treatment (CPT 1991b). It took some time to understand that inhumanity need not necessarily involve brutality or physical abuse of an individual or group of prisoners. Inhuman and degrading treatment can be caused simply by the conditions of captivity.

The European Court of Human Rights has delivered judgements which confirm this position. One example is the case of Peers v Greece (ECHR 2001), in which the court found that there had been a breach of Article 3 of the European Convention on Human Rights in the case of a pre-trial prisoner who was confined in a cell with no ventilation and no window and in which he had to use the toilet in the presence of another prisoner. Another example is the case of Kalashnikov v Russia (ECHR 2002), in which the court also found that there had been a breach of the Convention in the case of a prisoner who had been held in conditions of acute overcrowding in a cell where the light was constantly on and in which the dirty conditions led to the prisoner contracting skin diseases and fungal infections.

It should also be recognised that it is possible to have humanity in an environment with very poor physical conditions. The present author had an experience of this while visiting the Gambia a number of years ago. Given that prison conditions will very often reflect conditions in civil society, it is no surprise that the physical conditions in prisons in the Gambia are quite poverty stricken. In the main pre-trial prison in Banjul the group of visitors saw the dark and overcrowded conditions in which prisoners had to sleep and were invited to see the scarce resources elsewhere in the prison. At the end of the visit the prisoners gathered in the main yard of the prison and performed a concert for the visitors, who sat, along with the Commissioner of Prisons and other senior officials, on a raised platform. Towards the end of the concert the prisoners performed a traditional dance. Suddenly the Commissioner left his place among the guests and joined the prisoners in their energetic dancing. The prisoners welcomed him into their midst as though it were the most natural thing in the world, which for them it was. In that prison, despite the depressing physical conditions there was a sense of real humanity and empathy between staff and prisoners.

In contrast, in a number of developed countries physical conditions in prisons are generally satisfactory. The prisons are in a good state of repair and are clean and tidy. Each prisoner has his or her own cell and is reasonably well fed and clothed. Yet they are at best soulless institutions where there is little or no human interaction and at worst places of inhumanity where prisoners are not treated as human beings.

This underlines the key element that good prison management is to be found in a prison where there is a culture of decency and respect and where everyone is treated with humanity. There are a number of simple features which can be used as markers when assessing the extent to which such a culture exists or not in a prison. They are by and large the same indicators that one might use in any other human context. One which will be immediately obvious to the seasoned observer of prisons is the form of address used, particularly by staff towards prisoners. In many prison systems prisoners are given a personal number when they first come into prison. This is a number which will stay with each person until the day he or she leaves; it will be personal to the individual. If staff use this number rather than the proper name to address prisoners one can assume with some certainty that there is little humanity in such a setting. What happens more frequently is that prisoners are addressed merely by their surname although in return staff will expect to be given a title such as "Officer" or "Mister" before their name. If, on the other hand, this arrangement is reciprocal, if both parties are addressed formally as "Mister" or else informally by their given name, then there can be a reasonable expectation that there is at least a degree of mutual self respect within that prison.

Terminology is very important in the prison setting and the general use of language is often a good measure of humanity. This will obviously vary from language to language, but in English the description of meal times for prisoners as "feeding times" is more suggestive of a zoo than of a places where human beings eat. Similarly, when staff are escorting prisoners from one place to another one may well hear them referring to their charges as "bodies" or numbers to be passed from one point to the next rather than as people. All of this is indicative of a culture which regards prisoners as "a sub-species" of humanity (Narey 2001).

Good communications

An important feature of a well-managed prison is that it will have a good system for communications between everyone. Reference was made in the Introduction to the fact that in many hierarchical prison systems the only communication thought necessary is the passing of orders and instructions from the top of the organisation to the bottom. There is no upwards feedback and there is very little information passed across the organisation from one department to the other. This is not the mark of a well managed prison.

In chapter three we discussed the need for a balance between the different levels of responsibility of government ministers, national prison administrations and individual prisons, and the need for trust among those involved at different levels. The same principle applies within individual prisons. The prison director and senior management are responsible for overall management of the prison. The way they carry out their roles will be the main influence on the ethos within the prison. Their task is to provide a clear set of parameters within which the daily routine of the prison is to be exercised. They should then provide the support which encourages staff at other levels to carry out their daily tasks within these parameters. This should all be done in an atmosphere in which there is trust between everyone involved.

This will only happen if there is a good system of communications. In the first place, there has to be two way vertical communication. This means that there must be a process which permits senior management to have real dialogue with junior staff. This will include the ability of management to issue instructions when necessary in a manner which is understood by all staff. It will go further than that, since it will also enable management to seek the advice and opinion of staff, not only about issues of detail but also about more general matters of policy. This means that there must be a set of procedures which encourages junior staff to convey their views and opinions to senior management in a way which is transparent and which will not lay them open to criticism.

There must also be a good system of horizontal communication across the various departments in the prison. In a more traditional style, each department reports to the head of the prison and he or she then relays messages or instructions back down to other departments. In such a model, the different departments have no formal means of communicating with each other. This is likely to build in an unnecessary slowness and to increase the possibility of misunderstanding. There should be a forum which allows staff in the security department, the regimes and programmes department, the personnel department and the finance department to explain their different priorities to each other and to discover how their work can be complementary rather than in competition with that of other groups.

There should also be good channels of communication between prisoners and staff. There is no reason why prisoners should not be given the opportunity to express opinions about various aspects of prison life as it affects them. Obviously, some aspects of security and discipline may have to be excluded from such discussion, but there are many features of the prison which do not come into these categories.

It is important to recognise that a multi-layered communication system such as this will not undermine the discipline of the prison. On the contrary, it will make it more likely that staff at all levels will be more committed to their work and will have a better understanding of the change process. Similarly, prisoners will have an increased sense of security in their daily lives.

Treatment of visitors

Another important indicator of whether a prison is well managed is the manner in which visitors are treated, especially those who come to visit prisoners. There is a frequent temptation for prison officials to treat the family and friends of prisoners as if they too had broken the law and were liable to be subjected to supercilious treatment. The most obvious example of this is likely to occur when families come to visit the member who is in prison. More often than not the visitor will be female, a wife or a mother, who has travelled a considerable distance, perhaps with small children. Staff may keep them waiting for a long period before asking who they are or whom they have come to see. There may then be another interminable delay while the prisoner who is to be visited is located and brought to the visiting room. If the prison is a high security one the visitors, including small infants, may be subjected to intimate searching. In some cases this may be justified and indeed necessary on security grounds, but the manner in which it is carried out can be sensitive or insensitive depending on the approach taken by the member of staff. When the visit eventually begins the staff presence can be either discreet or over bearing. According to which of these two manners the staff adopt, the stress of the visit for both the prisoner and the visitors will be increased or decreased. None of this is to do with better or more lax security. It is solely a matter of the attitude of staff and the extent to which they regard visitors, let alone prisoners, as people who are to be shown the courtesies of normal human interaction.

This human face of the prison can be experienced even prior to arrival, if one has to make a telephone call to a prison. In some cases the telephone rings and rings until one is forced to give up in frustration. This is annoying enough if one is simply seeking general information. It is more serious if one is a legal adviser trying to make an appointment to visit a client. It is quite bewildering if one is a partner calling from a public telephone box to ask when one can visit the family member who is in prison.

Response in times of stress

Human relationships in a prison are, of course, multi-dimensional. It is not simply a question of how staff deal with prisoners and with visitors. Staff also are entitled to be treated with courtesy in return. However, in terms of relationships it is staff who undoubtedly hold the position of power and in that respect are able to set the tone of the prison, to which the prisoners can only respond.

This is particularly true in circumstances when tension is high between prisoners and staff, for example, in the wake of a serious incident such as a riot or in a prison with a tradition of poor interaction between staff and prisoners. In such prisons both groups are likely to have retreated to the safety of their respective traditions. Staff will hide behind formal rules and regulations and will avoid the informal contact with prisoners which is part and parcel of normal life in a prison. Similarly, in these situations prisoners will be reluctant to be seen talking to staff since this may be interpreted by other prisoners as disloyalty or, even worse, as passing on information to the enemy.

Serious incidents such as riots thankfully are not frequent occurrences in most prisons. In a well managed prison, where staff move among prisoners as a matter of course and have positive dealings with them, the causes which may give rise to a riot will usually be avoided. If trouble is brewing, it can usually be sensed in advance and steps can be taken to prevent it. However, even in the best managed prisons major incidents may occur occasionally. If this happens, it will be important to return to a semblance of normality as soon as possible after the incident is resolved. The initiative for taking the first step towards achieving this will almost invariably lie with staff. The present author has had personal experience of this when working in a high security prison where trust between staff and prisoners had completely broken down. The only way forward was to convince staff that they had to adopt a professional approach which combined proper security measures with a willingness to treat the prisoners in a humane way (Coyle 1994). This is the challenge which regularly faces staff who work in many high security prisons.

In considering these difficult issues one is reminded of a paragraph in a report written on the Marion Federal Penitentiary in the United States (Ward and Breed 1985):

> One of the greatest challenges to penal policy makers is the need to control the most violent prisoners in the country while at the same time exercising creativity in trying to devise and then try, on an experimental basis, activities that will not contribute to further deterioration of these inmates – deterioration which can lead in turn to greater risks of serious injury to staff, other prisoners, and often to the community upon the inmate's eventual release.

The way in which prison officials deal with the very small group of extremely violent prisoners, who refuse to conform to legitimate expectations, is one of the greatest challenges to the professionalism of prison staff.

A summary

In brief, a well managed prison is one in which the environment is decent and humane. In practical terms, these features can be measured by the quality of the human relationships between the prisoners who live there, the staff who work there and anyone who comes to visit for any reason. The principle is a very simple one. Its application is one of the most complex tasks in the field of good prison management.

The best managed prison systems are likely to be those which have a clear understanding of their objectives, mission and values. It has been suggested in this book that there are at least three key sets of processes, each of which is linked to the other. The first is a series of system issues, including links with other parts of the criminal justice process and public sector agencies. The second is a series of structural issues about how the service is organised so as to recognise its hierarchical nature while at the same time encouraging staff to develop their full potential and use their initiative. The third, which follows from the first two, is a series of what can be called people issues, to do with leadership and the management of all those involved in the system, particularly staff and prisoners. If these processes can be dealt with in the manner which has been described there will be a high possibility that the outcome will be good prison management.

Crucial to all of this is a good communication system, which goes up and down and across the organisation. Staff at all levels have to be aware of, and subscribe to, the mission and values of the organisation. They have to understand policy decisions, whether they emanate from national headquarters or from local management. They must also feel that they can be heard and will be listened to when they wish to contribute to the thinking and development of the organisation.

Finally, it has to be recognised that good prison management is dynamic. It is a continuous process rather than something which can be achieved once and for all and, very importantly, that it is a means to an end rather than an end in itself. To express this in different terms, it is a journey which never ends. If it ever does come to an end, that will simply be an indication that the culture of the prison has ceased to be dynamic and changing, and instead has become fossilised, no longer alive. This journey can without doubt be a dangerous one at times. It implies a degree of uncertainty, a recognition of the need to change. Prisons as organisations do not like uncertainty; they see it as destabilising and threatening. That is why they need to be set in the context of an agreed set of ethical values linked to clear leadership. If that is the case, the change process will lead to better managed prisons, which are more secure, safer and more effective; in which there is a respect for decency and humanity.

References and bibliography

Adler M and Longhurst B, 1994. *Discourse, Power and Justice: Towards a New Sociology of Imprisonment*. Routledge: London.

Amnesty International, 2002. Available online at http://web.amnesty.org/rmp/dplibrary.nsf

Boin A, 1998. *Contrasts in Leadership: An Institutional Study of Two Prison Systems*. Eburon: Delft.

2001. *Crafting Public Institutions: Leadership in two Prison Systems*. Lynne Rienner: London.

Carnall C, 1992. *Managing Change: Self Development for Managers*. Routledge, London.

Carroll L, 1999. *Lawful Order: A Case Study of Correctional Crisis and Reform*. Garland: New York.

Chesney-Lind M, 'Building more prisons won't make Hawaii better' February 6, 1998, *Honolulu Star-Bulletin* at http://starbulletin.com/98/02/11/editorial/viewpointf.html

Civil Liberties Organisation, 1996. *Behind the Wall: A Report on Prison Conditions in Nigeria*. Civil Liberties Organisation: Lagos.

Clegg C K N and Legge K (eds.), 1985. *Case Studies in Organisational Behaviour*, Harper Row: London.

Connor P E and Lake L K, 1988. *Managing Organisational Change*. Praeger: New York.

Clemmer D, 1965. *The Prison Community*. Holt, Rinehart and Winston: New York.

Cloward R A., 1960. *Theoretical Studies in Social Organisation of the Prison*. (1975 reprint). Social Science Research Council, Kraus Reprint: New York.

Council of Europe, 1983. *Prison Information Bulletin*. Number 2, December 1983. Council of Europe: Strasbourg.

1987. *European Prison Rules*. Recommendation No. R(87)3 adopted by the Committee of Ministers of the Council of Europe on 12 February 1987. Strasbourg.

1991a. *Report to the United Kingdom Government on the visit to the United Kingdom carried out by the European Committee for the Prevention of Torture and Inhuman or Degrading Treatment or Punishment (CPT) from 29 July 1990 to 10 August 1990*. Council of Europe: Strasbourg. CPT/ Inf. (91) 15 [EN].

1991b. *Response of the United Kingdom Government to the report of the European Committee for the Prevention of Torture and Inhuman or Degrading Treatment or Punishment (CPT) on its visit to the United Kingdom from 29 July to 10 August 1990.* Council of Europe: Strasbourg. CPT/ Inf. (91) 16 [EN].

1998. *Report to the Government of the Netherlands on the visit to the Netherlands Antilles carried out by the European Committee for the Prevention of Torture and Inhuman or Degrading Treatment or Punishment (CPT) from 7 to 11 December 1997.* Council of Europe: Strasbourg. CPT/ Inf. (98) 17 [EN] (Part 1).

1999a, *Interim report of the Dutch Government in response to the report of the European Committee for the Prevention of Torture and Inhuman or Degrading Treatment or Punishment (CPT) on its visit to the Netherlands from 17 to 27 November 1997.* Council of Europe: Strasbourg. CPT/Inf. (99) 5 [EN].

1999b, *Report to the Hungarian Government on the visit to Hungary carried out by the European Committee for the Prevention of Torture and Inhuman or Degrading Treatment or Punishment (CPT) from 5 to 16 December 1999.* Council of Europe: Strasbourg. CPT/Inf. (2001) 2 [EN].

1999c, *Report to the Icelandic Government on the visit to Iceland carried out by the European Committee for the Prevention of Torture and Inhuman or Degrading Treatment or Punishment (CPT) from 29 March to 6 April 1998.* Council of Europe: Strasbourg. CPT/Inf. (99) 1 [EN].

2001 *Council of Europe Annual Penal Statistics SPACE I: 2000 enquiry on prison populations.* Pierre Victor Tournier Strasbourg, 23 January 2001 pc-cp\space\documents\pc-cp (2001) 2 – e PC-CP (2001) 2

Coyle A, 1991. *Inside: Rethinking Scotland's Prisons.* Scottish Child: Edinburgh.

1994. *The Prisons We Deserve.* Harper Collins: London.

1999. 'Prison Reform and the Management of TB in Eastern Europe and Central Asia'. In *Stern*, 1999b.

2002. *A Human Rights Approach to Prison Management: Handbook for Prison Staff.* ICPS: London

2003. With Campbell, Allison and Neufeld, Rodney, (eds.), *Capitalist Punishment: Prison Privatisation & Human Rights.* Clarity Press: Atlanta.

Cressey D R (ed.), 1966. *The Prison: Studies in Institutional Organisation and Change.* Holt, Reinhart & Winston: New York.

Department of Corrections, 2001. Annual Report, 1 July 2000 to 30 June 2001. Department of Corrections: Wellington.

Department for International Development (DFID) 2000. *Issues - Justice and Poverty Reduction: Safety, Security and Access to Justice for All.* DFID: London.

DiIulio J J Jnr, 1987. *Governing Prisons: A Comparative Study of Correctional Management.* Free Press: New York.

Dostoyevsky F M, 1866. *Crime and Punishment.* Penguin Classics, 1996, Penguin: USA.

Duguid S, 2000. *Can Prisons Work? The Prisoner as Object and Subject in Modern Corrections.* University of Toronto Press: Canada.

Etzioni A, 1969. *A Sociological Reader in Complex Organisations.* Holt, Rinehart and Winston: New York.

ECHR 2001. Case of Peers v Greece. Application 28524/95. Judgement 19.4.2001. Available at http://hudoc.echr.coe.int/hudoc

ECHR 2002. Case of Kalashnikov v Russia. Application 47095/99. Judgement 15.7.2002. Available at http://hudoc.echr.coe.int/hudoc

Grew B D, 1958. *Prison Governor.* Herbert Jenkins: London.

Home Office, 1910. *Parliamentary Debates Official Reports (Hansard) House of Commons First Session of the Twenty-ninth Parliament of the United Kingdom of Great Britain and Ireland. Sixth Volume of Session (Comprising period from 11th July 1910 to Wednesday 3rd August 1910).* HMSO: London.

   1991. *Report of an Inquiry into Prison Disturbances April 1990.* (Woolf Report) Cm 456. HMSO: London.

   1999. *Criminal Statistics England and Wales 1999.* Cm. 5001. HMSO: London.

   1999. *Digest 4: Information on the Criminal Justice System in England and Wales.* Home Office: London.

   2001. *Prison Statistics England and Wales 2000.* Cm. 5250. HMSO: London.

Hood R, 1996. *The Death Penalty: A World-wide Perspective (Revised and Updated Edition).* Clarendon Press: Oxford.

Jacobs J, 1977. *Stateville: The Penitentiary in Mass Society.* University of Chicago Press: Chicago.

Kauffman K, 1988. *Prison Officers and their World.* Harvard University Press: Cambridge, MA.

King R D, 1999. 'The rise and rise of supermax: An American solution in search of a problem?' in *Punishment and Society: The International Journal of Penology.* Volume One, Number 2, October 1999. Sage: London.

Lewis D, 1997. *Hidden Agendas: Politics; Law and Disorder.* Hamish Hamilton: London.

Liebling A and Price D, 2001. *The Prison Officer.* Prison Service Journal: Leyhill.

Lombardo L X, 1989. *Guards Imprisoned: Correctional Officers at Work.* Elsevier: New York.

Lygo R, 1991. *Management of the Prison Service.* Home Office: London.

Mandela N, 1994. *Long Walk to Freedom: The Autobiography of Nelson Mandela.* Little, Brown: London.

Matsunaga Senator M, 2000. *Minutes of Regular Meeting of the Kaimuki Neighborhood Board.* Wednesday September 6, 2000. Available online at http://www.co.honolulu.hi.us/nco/nb4/00/4sepmin.htm

McCleery R H, 1957. 'Policy Change in Prison Management' in *Etzioni* (1969).

McConville S, 1981. *A History of English Prison Administration: Volume One 1750-1877.* Routledge and Kegan Paul: London.

McDevitt T M and Rowe P M, 2002. *The United States in International Comparison: Census 2000 Brief.* United States Bureau of the Census. C2KBR/- 01-11. Available online at www.census.gov/prod/2002pubs/c2kbr01-11.pdf

Miller A, 1976. *Inside Outside: The Story of a Prison Governor.* Queensgate Press: London.

Moczydlowski P, 1992. *The Hidden Life of Polish Prisons.* Indiana University Press: Bloomington.

Monterey County Civil Grand Jury, 2000. *Final Report January 3, 2000: Special Report - Overcrowding At Salinas Valley State Prison* Available online at www.co.monterey.ca.us/court/grand_jury_report_1999/overcr.htm

Narey M, 2001. Speech to Prison Service Annual Conference, 5th February 2001. Available online at http://www.hmprisonservice.gov.uk/

Office of Population Censuses and Surveys (OPCS), 1985. *Staff Attitudes in the Prison Service.* HMSO: London.

Prison Service, 1992. *Occupation of Prisons, Remand Centres, Young Offender Institutions and Police Cells on 31 December 1992.* Prison Service: London.

Reynolds J and Smart U (eds.), 1996. Prison Policy and Practice: 35 Years of the Prison Service Journal. *Prison Service Journal*: Great Britain.

Rich C E F, 1932. *Recollections of a Prison Governor.* Hurst and Blackett: London.

Rock P, 1996. *Reconstructing a Women's Prison: The Holloway Redevelopment Project, 1968-88.* Clarendon Press: Oxford.

Ruck S K, (ed.), 1951. *Paterson on Prisons: Being the Collected Papers of Sir Alexander Paterson.* Frederick Muller: London.

Scottish Prison Service, 1988. *Custody and Care: Policy and Plans for the Scottish Prison Service.* HMSO: Edinburgh.

1990. *Opportunity and Responsibility: Developing New Approaches to the Management of the Long Term Prison System in Scotland.* Scottish Prison Service: Edinburgh.

1991. *Organising for Excellence.* Scottish Prison Service: Edinburgh.

Sentencing Project, 2002. *Facts about Prisons and Prisoners.* Available online at http://www.sentencingproject.org/brief/pub1035.pdf

Shankardass R D (ed.), 2000. *Punishment and the Prison: Indian and International Perspectives.* Sage Publications: New Delhi.

Solzhenitsyn A I, 1974. *Gulag Archipelago, 1918-1956: An Experiment in Literary Investigation.* Wm Collins & Co Ltd: Glasgow

Sparks R F, Bottoms A and Hay W, 1996. *Prisons and the Problem of Order.* Clarendon Press: Oxford.

Stern V, 1987. *Bricks of Shame – Britain's Prisons.* Penguin: Middlesex.

1998. *A Sin Against the Future: Imprisonment in the World.* Penguin: Middlesex.

1999a. *Alternatives to Prison in Developing Countries.* International Centre for Prison Studies: London.

(ed.) 1999b. *Sentenced to Die? The Problem of TB in Prisons in Eastern Europe and Central Asia.* International Centre for Prison Studies: London.

Sykes G M, 1958. *The Society of Captives: A Study of Maximum Security Prison.* Princeton University Press: Princeton.

Thomas J E, 1972. *The English Prison Officer Since 1850: a Study in Conflict.* Routledge: London.

United Nations 1957. *Standard Minimum Rules for the Treatment of Prisoners.* Adopted by the First United Nations Congress on the Prevention of Crime and the Treatment of Offenders, held at Geneva in 1955, and approved by the Economic and Social Council by its resolution 663 C (XXIV) of 31 July 1957 and 2076 (LXII) of 13 May 1977.

1979. *Code of Conduct for Law Enforcement Officials.* Adopted by General Assembly resolution 34/169 of 17 December 1979.

1985. *Standard Minimum Rules for the Administration of Juvenile Justice ("The Beijing Rules").* Adopted by General Assembly resolution 40/33 of 29 November 1985.

1988. *Body of Principles for the Protection of All Persons under Any Form of Detention or Imprisonment.* Adopted by General Assembly resolution 43/173 of 9 December 1988.

1990. *Basic Principles for the Treatment of Prisoners.* Adopted and proclaimed by General Assembly resolution 45/111 of 14 December 1990.

1990. *Rules for the Protection of Juveniles Deprived of their Liberty.* Adopted by General Assembly resolution 45/113 of 14 December 1990.

UNHCHR, 2000. *Manual on Human Rights Training for Prison Officials.* Office of the United Nations High Commissioner for Human Rights: Geneva.

United States Bureau of Justice Statistics, 1995. *Bulletin: Prisoners in 1994.*

2002. *Bulletin: Prisoners in 2001.* Available at http://www.ojp.usdoj.gov/bjs/

United States Department of Justice, Office of Public Affairs, 1997. 'Jails in Maricopa County, Arizona to take steps to reduce excessive Force and Use of Improper Restraints' *Press Release* Number 451: 31 October 1997. Available online at http://www.usdoj.gov/

Van Zyl Smit D and Dünkel F, 2001. *Imprisonment Today and Tomorrow - International Perspectives on Prisoners' Rights and Prison Conditions.* 2nd edition. Kluwer Law International: The Hague.

Walmsley R, 2001. *World Prison Population: Facts, Trends and Solutions - Statistical Overview of World Imprisonment.* Paper presented to the United Nations Programme Network Institutes Technical Assistance Workshop in Vienna, Austria May 10, 2001. Available online at www.unicri.it

2002. *Research Findings 166: World Prison Population List (third edition)* Home Office: UK.

Ward D and Breed A, 1985. Report on the US Penitentiary Marion, presented to the Committee on the Judiciary of the US House of Representatives. US Government Printing Office: Washington.

Lord Wilberforce in *Raymond* v *Honey* [1982] 1 All ER 756 at 759.

Williamson H E, 1990. *The Corrections Profession.* Sage: London.

Wilson D and Bryans S, 1998. *The Prison Governor: Theory and Practice.* Prison Service Journal: Leyhill.

World Prison Brief, 2002. Available online at http://www.prisonstudies.org

Wozniak E, Dyson G and Carnie J, 1998. *The Third Prison Survey.* Scottish Prison Service Occasional Paper No. 3. Scottish Prison Service: Edinburgh.

Index